First edition April 2013

Published by Design Community College Inc,

Design Community College Inc.
PO Box 1153
Topanga CA 90290 USA

info@curedale.com
Designed and illustrated by Robert Curedale

ISBN-10: 0989246825
ISBN-13: 978-0-9892468-2-8

Structured Workshops
The author presents workshops online and in person in global locations for executives, engineers, designers, technology professionals and anyone interested in learning and applying these proven innovation methods. For information contact: info@curedale.com

Mapping Methods

for design and strategy

Robert Curedale

dedicated to aidan and liam

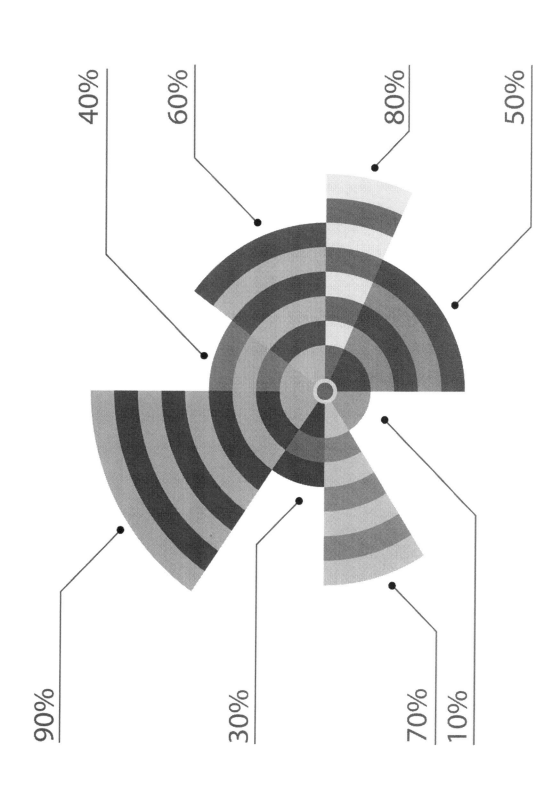

contents

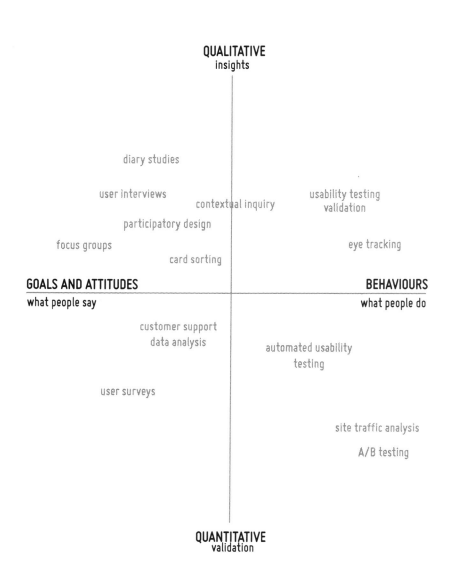

QUALITATIVE
insights

diary studies

user interviews

usability testing
validation

contextual inquiry

participatory design

focus groups

eye tracking

card sorting

GOALS AND ATTITUDES

what people say

BEHAVIOURS

what people do

customer support
data analysis

automated usability
testing

user surveys

site traffic analysis

A/B testing

QUANTITATIVE
validation

Source: after Mulder

introduction

Mapping methods are used by teams to develop strategy to assist a wide variety of activities. Mapping methods are particularly useful for:

1. Make informed design decisions
2. Identify areas of opportunity for developing new products, services and experiences
3. Analyzing a competitive landscape
4. To understand trends
5. To analyze complex, changing and ambiguous design problems
6. Look for areas where there are ideal factors to support a product or service.
7. Look for areas without competitive rivals
8. Enable meaningful conversations about difficult design topics
9. Use real-time information to help identify potential problems and make the best decisions
10. Create design that has a better return on investment
11. Understand your customer's perspectives
12. Create more successful design.

Mapping methods can be applied to support informed design decisions as part of a Design Thinking approach to design. Design Thinking is an approach to designing products, services, architecture, spaces and experiences that is being quickly adopted by designers, architects and some of the world's leading brands such as GE, Target, SAP, Procter and Gamble, IDEO and Intuit. It is being taught at leading universities including Stanford and Harvard. Design Thinking creates practical and innovative solutions to problems. It drives repeatable innovation and business value. Design Thinking can be used to develop a wide range of products, services, experiences and strategy. It is an approach that can be applied by anyone.

This book is an indispensable reference guide for:
1. Architects, industrial designers, interior designers, UX and web designers,
2. service designers, exhibit designers, design educators and students, visual communication designers, packaging and fashion designers, all types of designers
3. Engineers and Marketing professionals
4. Executives and senior business leaders
5. Decision makers in R&D of products, services, systems and experiences
6. School teachers and school students

ACTORS MAP

ACTIVITY STAGE

Leave

Engage

Travel

Anticpate

Internet

Mobile

Face to Face

Mobile

ACTORS

TOUCHPOINTS

INTERACTIONS

1

2

3

4

NOTES

1. **Activity Stage.** This is the timeline of stages in the activity that you are presenting

2. **Actors.** Each icon represents a person or stakeholder or group or organization involved in the activity at that particular stage

3. **Interactions.** This is the type of interaction such as face to face, mobile or online.

4. **Touchpoints.** Customer interaction channels such as call centers, web sites, automated teller machines and web kiosks.

actors map

WHAT IS IT?
The Actors Map represents the system of stakeholders and their relationships. It is a view of the service and its context. Stakeholders are organized by their function.

WHY USE THIS METHOD?
1. Understanding relationships is an important aspect of service design.

CHALLENGES
1. This is not a user centered method

WHY USE THIS METHOD?
1. Inexpensive and fast.
2. Connects to existing research tools and methods
3. Makes implicit knowledge explicit
4. Structures complex reality
5. Flexible for use in different contexts.

WHEN TO USE THIS METHOD
1. Know Context
2. Know User
3. Frame insights

SEE ALSO
1. Network map.

REFERENCES
1. (2007) Nicola Morelli, New representation techniques for designing in a systemic perspective, paper presented at Design Inquires, Stockholm.

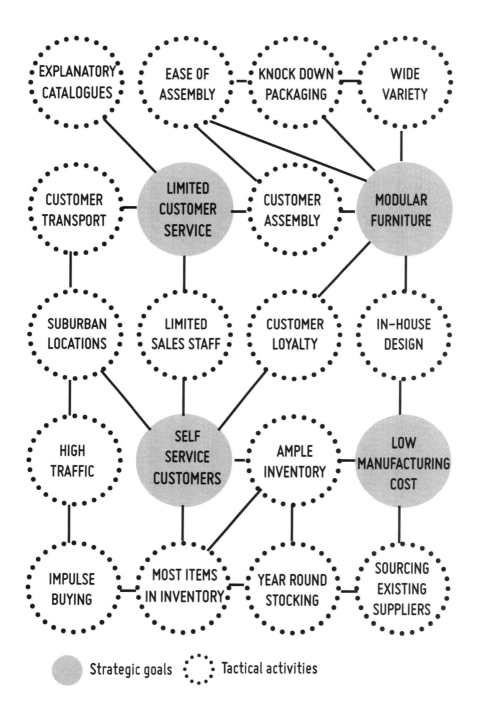

Activity map for Ikea (after Porter)

activity map

WHAT IS IT?

An activity map is a map that show a companies strategic position in relation to company activities. A number of higher order strategic themes are implemented through linked activities.

WHO INVENTED IT?

Walt Disney Corporation 1957

WHY USE THIS METHOD?

1. Activity maps are useful for understanding and strengthening organizational strategy.
2. The value of individual activities cannot be separated from the system of activities.
3. Helps develop a unique competitive position.
4. Helps align activities with strategy
5. Helps understand trade off and choices.

WHEN TO USE THIS METHOD

1. Define intent
2. Know Context
3. Know User
4. Frame insights

HOW TO USE THIS METHOD

1. Is each activity contributing positively to the overall strategy, and customer needs?
2. Are there ways of making the activities and the relationships of activities support strategy better?

REFERENCES

1. Michael E Porter. What is Strategy? Harvard Business Review November–December 1996

BAR CHART

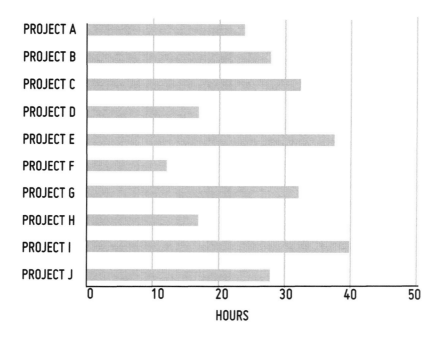

bar chart

WHAT IS IT?

A simple bar chart is useful to present information for a quick problem or opportunity analysis. It provides a comparison of quantities of items or frequencies of events within a particular time period.

WHO INVENTED IT?

The first bar graph appeared in the 1786 book The Commercial and Political Atlas, by William Playfair (1759-1823)

WHY USE THIS METHOD?

1. To display a "snapshot" comparison of categories.
2. To depict the relationship between variations over time.
3. To illustrate process variability or trends.
4. To indicate a potential problem area (high or low frequencies).

Challenges

1. Care should be taken not to insert more than five bars or cover more than five time periods. This would make the Bar Chart cluttered and difficult to interpret.

When to use this method

1. Frame insights

HOW TO USE THIS METHOD

1. Collect data from sources
2. Draw the vertical and horizontal axes.
3. Decide on the scale
4. Draw a bar for each item.
5. Label the axes

RESOURCES

1. Pen
2. Paper
3. Graph paper
4. Computer
5. Graphics software

REFERENCES

1. Kelley, W. M.; Donnelly, R. A. (2009) The Humongous Book of Statistics Problems. New York, NY: Alpha Books ISBN 1592578659

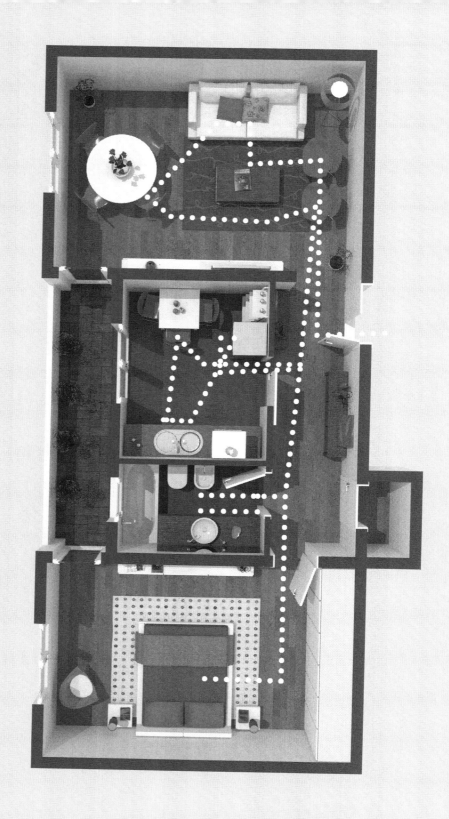

behavioral map

WHAT IS IT?

Behavioral mapping is a method used to record and analyze human activities in a location. This method is used to document what participants are doing and time spent at locations and travelling. Behavioral maps can be created based on a person or a space

WHO INVENTED IT?

Ernest Becker 1962

WHY USE THIS METHOD?

1. This method helps develop an understanding of space layouts, interactions and experiences and behaviors.
2. Helps understand way finding.
3. Helps optimize use of space.
4. A limitation of this method is that motivations remain unknown.
5. Use when you want to develop more efficient or effective use of space in retail environments, exhibits, architecture and interior design.

WHEN TO USE THIS METHOD

1. Define intent
2. Know Context
3. Know User
4. Frame insights
5. Explore Concepts

HOW TO USE THIS METHOD

1. Decide who are the users.
2. Ask what is the purpose of the space?
3. Consider what behaviors are meaningful.
4. Consider different personas.
5. Participants can be asked to map their use of a space on a floor plan and can be asked to reveal their motivations.
6. Can use shadowing or video ethnographic techniques.
7. Create behavioral map.
8. Analyze behavioral map.
9. Reorganize space based on insights.

RESOURCES

1. A map of the space.
2. Video camera
3. Digital still camera
4. Notebook
5. Pens

REFERENCES

1. Nickerson 1993: Bnet. Understanding your consumers through behavioral mapping.
2. A Practical Guide to Behavioral Research Tools and Techniques. Fifth Edition Robert Sommer and Barbara Sommer ISBN13: 9780195142099ISBN10: 0195142098 Aug 2001

BENEFITS MAP

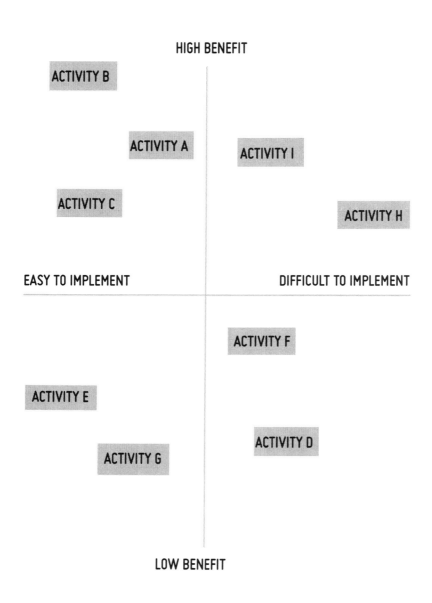

HIGH BENEFIT

ACTIVITY B

ACTIVITY A

ACTIVITY I

ACTIVITY C

ACTIVITY H

EASY TO IMPLEMENT

DIFFICULT TO IMPLEMENT

ACTIVITY F

ACTIVITY E

ACTIVITY D

ACTIVITY G

LOW BENEFIT

benefits map

WHAT IS IT?

The benefits map is a simple tool that helps your team decide what will give you the best return on investment for time invested

WHY USE THIS METHOD?

1. Aids communication and discussion within the organization.
2. It is human nature to do tasks which are not most urgent first.
3. To gain competitive advantage.
4. Helps build competitive strategy
5. Helps build communication strategy
6. Helps manage time effectively

CHALLENGES

1. Can be subjective

WHEN TO USE THIS METHOD

1. Know Context
2. Know User
3. Frame insights
4. Explore Concepts

HOW TO USE THIS METHOD

1. Moderator draws axes on whiteboard or flip chart.
2. Worthwhile activity at the start of a project.
3. Map individual tasks.
4. Interpret the map.
5. Create strategy.
6. Tasks which have high benefit with low investment may be given priority.

RESOURCES

1. Pen
2. Paper
3. White board
4. Dry erase markers

benjamin franklin method

WHAT IS IT?
A method developed by Benjamin Franklin for making decisions.

WHO INVENTED IT?
Benjamin Franklin 1772

WHY USE THIS METHOD?
1. It is simple
2. It was developed and used by Benjamin Franklin who was a successful decision maker.

WHEN TO USE THIS METHOD
1. Explore Concepts

RESOURCES
1. Pen
2. Paper
3. White board
4. Dry erase markers
5. Post-it-notes

HOW TO USE THIS METHOD
Quote from a letter from Benjamin Franklin to Joseph Priestley London, September 19, 1772

"To get over this, my Way is, to divide half a Sheet of Paper by a Line into two Columns, writing over the one Pro, and over the other Con. Then during three or four Days Consideration I put down under the different Heads short Hints of the different Motives that at different Times occur to me for or against the Measure. When I have thus got them all together in one View, I endeavour to estimate their respective Weights; and where I find two, one on each side, that seem equal, I strike them both out: If I find a Reason pro equal to some two Reasons con, I strike out the three. If I judge some two Reasons con equal to some three Reasons pro, I strike out the five; and thus proceeding I find at length where the Ballance lies; and if after a Day or two of farther Consideration nothing new that is of Importance occurs on either side, I come to a Determination accordingly.

And tho' the Weight of Reasons cannot be taken with the Precision of Algebraic Quantities, yet when each is thus considered separately and comparatively, and the whole lies before me, I think I can judge better, and am less likely to take a rash Step; and in fact I have found great Advantage from this kind of Equation, in what may be called Moral or Prudential Algebra"

ACTIVITY PHASE	ACTIVITY PHASE	ACTIVITY PHASE	ACTIVITY PHASE	ACTIVITY PHASE	ACTIVITY PHASE

CUSTOMER ACTIONS

What does user do?

TOUCHPOINTS

moments places customer contact

LINE OF INTERACTION

DIRECT CONTACT

What your Staff do

LINE OF VISIBILITY

BACK OFFICE

What your Staff do

EMOTIONAL EXPERIENCE

+

−

blueprint

WHAT IS IT?

A blueprint is a process map often used to describe the delivery of services information is presented as a number of parallel rows of activities. These are sometimes called swim lanes. They may document activities over time such as:

1. Customer Actions
2. Touch points
3. Direct Contact visible to customers
4. Invisible back office actions
5. Support Processes
6. Physical Evidence
7. Emotional Experience for customer.

WHO INVENTED IT?

Lynn Shostack 1983

WHEN TO USE THIS METHOD

1. Know Context
2. Know User
3. Frame insights

WHY TO USE THIS METHOD

1. Can be used for design or improvement of existing services or experiences.
2. Is more tangible than intuition.
3. Makes the process of service development more efficient.
4. A common point of reference for stakeholders for planning and discussion.
5. Tool to assess the impact of change.

HOW TO USE THIS METHOD

1. Define the service or experience to focus on.
2. A blueprint can be created in a brainstorming session with stakeholders.
3. Define the customer demographic.
4. See though the customer's eyes.
5. Define the activities and phases of activity under each heading.
6. Link the contact or customer touchpoints to the needed support functions
7. Use post-it-notes on a white board for initial descriptions and rearrange as necessary drawing lines to show the links.
8. Create the blueprint then refine iteratively.

RESOURCES

1. Paper
2. Pens
3. White board
4. Dry-erase markers
5. Camera
6. Blueprint templates
7. Post-it-notes

REFERENCES

1. (1991) G. Hollins, W. Hollins, Total Design: Managing the design process in the service sector, Trans Atlantic Publications
2. (2004) R. Kalakota, M.Robinson, Services Blueprint: Roadmap for Execution, Addison-Wesley, Boston.

BOWMAN'S STRATEGY CLOCK

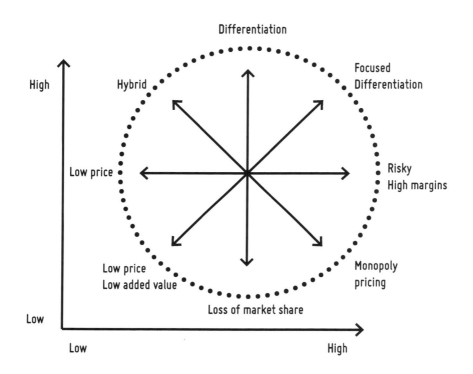

bowman's strategy clock

WHAT IS IT?

This is a method for analyzing the possibility of success for a number of different strategies. It identifies the cost and perceived value of different approaches. Bowman's Strategy Clock has eight alternative strategies in four quadrants.

WHO INVENTED IT?

Cliff Bowman and David Faulkner 1996

WHY USE THIS METHOD?

1. Helps develop a strategy of competitive advantage.
2. Can be used to analyze current strategy and strategies of competitors.

RESOURCES

1. Pen
2. Paper
3. White board
4. Dry erase markers

WHEN TO USE THIS METHOD

1. Define intent

HOW TO USE THIS METHOD

1. Graph competing options on a two axis chart
2. The x axis is high low price
3. The y axis is high low perceived value to the consumer
4. The 8 types of strategy are
   ◦ Low price low value
   ◦ Low price
   ◦ Moderate price and differentiation
   ◦ Differentiation
   ◦ Focused differentiation
   ◦ Increased price and standard product
   ◦ High price low value
   ◦ Low value and standard price.
   ◦ Some of these alternatives are not viable strategies in a competitive environment.

REFERENCES

1. Bowman, C. and Faulkner, D. (1997), "Competitive and Corporate Strategy", Irwin, London.

C-BOX

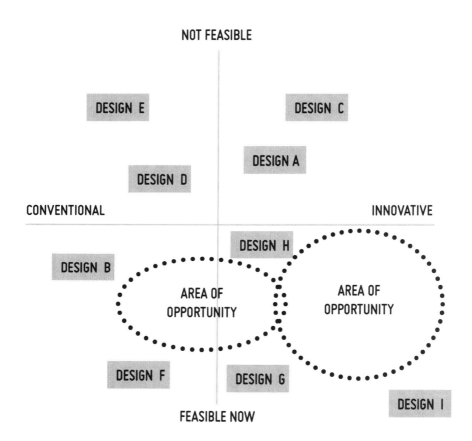

c-box

WHAT IS IT?

A c-box is a type of perceptual map that allows comparison and evaluation of a large number of ideas generated in a brainstorming session by a design team. The method allows everyone to contribute in a democratic way. It can be used to identify the most feasible and innovative ideas. It is up to your team to decide the level of innovation that they would like to carry forward from the idea generation or divergent phase of the project to the convergent or refinement and implementation phases.

WHO INVENTED IT?

Marc Tassoul, Delft 2009

WHY USE THIS METHOD?

1.   It is democratic
2.   It is quick and productive
3.   It is inexpensive

WHEN TO USE THIS METHOD

1.   Frame insights
2.   Explore Concepts

REFERENCES

Tassoul, M. (2006) Creative Facilitation: a Delft Approach, Delft: VSSD.

HOW TO USE THIS METHOD

1.   The moderator defines the design problem
2.   You group can be optimally from 4 to 20 people.
3.   On a white board or large sheet of paper create two axes. You can also use tape on a large wall.
4.   The team should sit around a table facing the wall.
5.   Innovation on the horizontal and feasibility on the vertical axes creating 4 quadrants
6.   The scale on the innovation ranges from not innovative at the left hand to highly innovative on the right hand end.
7.   Alternative axes are attractiveness and functionality.
8.   The scale for feasibility runs from not feasible now at the bottom to immediately feasible at the top.
9.   Hand out ten post-it-notes to each member of your team.
10.   Brainstorm concepts. Each team member to generate 5 to 10 concepts over 30 minutes. One idea per post-it note. Hand out more post-it notes if required.
11.   Concepts can be simple sketches or written ideas or a combination of the two.
12.   Each team member then presents each idea taking one to three minutes per idea depending on time available.
13.   With the group's input discuss the ideas and precise position on the map.
14.   Position each post-it-note according to the group consensus.

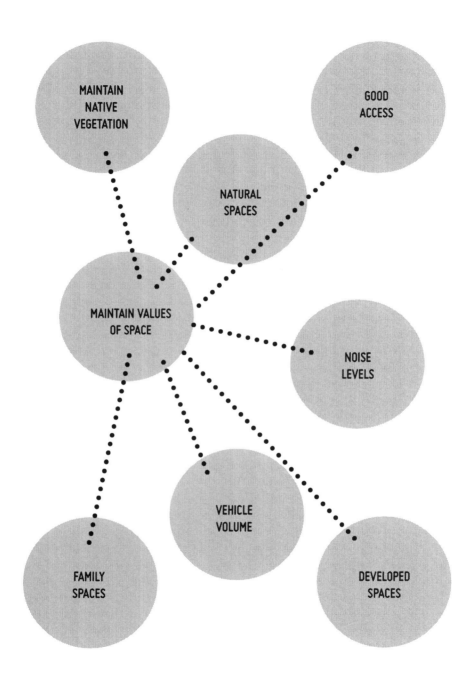

cognitive map

WHAT IS IT?

A cognitive map is a mental map of an environment. Cognitive maps are a method by which people remember and recall a physical or virtual environment and spatial knowledge.

WHO INVENTED IT?

Edward Tolman 1948.
Trowbridge 1913

WHY USE THIS METHOD?

1. Useful to discover how people navigate in a real or virtual space.
2. Used to understand a problem space.
3. Cognitive maps uncover how people make decisions.
4. Cognitive maps uncover how people perceive spaces

WHEN TO USE THIS METHOD

1. Know Context
2. Know User
3. Frame insights
4. Explore Concepts

HOW TO USE THIS METHOD

1. Ask a subject to create a map showing how they navigate in a real or a virtual space.
2. Select participants
3. Ask the participant to describe how they get to a location and how they return referencing the obstacles.
4. Maps can be created by a group of people to incorporate different viewpoints.

RESOURCES

1. Note pad
2. Paper
3. Pens
4. Video camera

REFERENCES

5. Eden, C. (1992). On the nature of cognitive maps. Journal of Management Studies, 29, 261–265.
6. Kitchin RM (1994). "Cognitive Maps: What Are They and Why Study Them?". Journal of Environmental Psychology 14 (1): 1—19. DOI:10.1016/S0272-4944(05)80194-X.
1. Tolman E.C. (July 1948). "Cognitive maps in rats and men". Psychological Review 55 (4): 189—208. DOI:10.1037/h0061626. PMID 18870876.

COMMUNICATIONS MAP

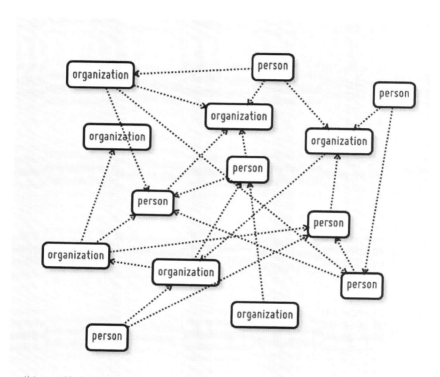

It is possible to show existing and planned relationships on your communications map

communications map

WHAT IS IT?

A communications map is a tool to study and create strategy for communications. It may be used in a project to understand where there are gaps which could affect the project outcomes. The project communication map processes documents the critical links among people and information that are necessary for successful project outcomes.

WHY USE THIS METHOD?

1. It may show where there are gaps in communications which need to be addressed.
2. Assists the project team to provide timely and accurate information to all stakeholders.

WHEN TO USE THIS METHOD

1. Know Context
2. Know User
3. Frame insights

RESOURCES

1. Pens
2. Paper
3. White board
4. Dry-erase markers

HOW TO USE THIS METHOD

1. Identify stakeholders.
2. Identify those with whom
3. Your organization needs the strongest communications linkages.
4. Identify Internal audiences.
5. Identify Peer groups or sub groups.
6. Identify Strong and frequent communications
7. Connectivity needed to a primary audience.
8. Identify less frequent communications connectivity needed to a secondary audience.
9. Determine stakeholder needs.
10. Identify communication methods and resources.
11. Prepare communication map showing existing and desired communications.
12. Distribute to stakeholders for feedback.
13. Incorporate Changes
14. Implement.

CONTEXT MAP

	TRENDS	UNCERTAINTIES	TECHNOLOGY	USER NEEDS	ECONOMIC	POLITICAL	TRENDS

context map

WHAT IS IT?

A context map is a tool for representing complex factors affecting an organization or design visually. Context maps are sometimes used by directors or organizations as a tool to enable discussion of the effects of change and related interacting business, cultural and environmental factors in order to create a strategic vision for an organization. A context map can be used to analyze trends

WHO INVENTED IT?

Joseph D. Novak Cornell University 1970s.

WHY USE THIS METHOD?

Uses include:
1. New knowledge creation
2. Documenting the knowledge existing informally within an organization.
3. Creating a shared strategic vision

WHEN TO USE THIS METHOD

1. Define intent
2. Know Context
3. Know User
4. Frame insights

RESOURCES

1. Template
2. White board
3. Paper flip chart
4. Pens
5. Dry-erase markers
6. Post-it-notes

HOW TO USE THIS METHOD

1. Put together a team of between 4 and 20 participants with diverse backgrounds and outlooks.
2. Appoint a good moderator
3. Prepare a space. Use a private room with a white board or large wall.
4. Distribute post-it notes to each participant.
5. Brainstorm the list of factors one at a time.
6. These can include Trends, technology, trends, political factors, economic climate customer needs, uncertainties.
7. Each participant can contribute.
8. All contributions are recorded on the white board or on the wall with the post-it-notes.
9. When all factors have been discussed prioritize each group of contributions to identify the most critical.
10. This can be done by rearranging the post-it-notes or white board notes.
11. Video the session and photograph the notes after the session.
12. Analyze the map and create strategy.

REFERENCES

1. Context Map: A Method to Represent the Interactions Between Students' Learning and Multiple Context Factors written by Gyoungho Lee and Lei Bao Physics Education Research Conference 2002

CRITICAL SUCCESS FACTOR CHART

FACTOR   BRAND

Factor	A -	A +	A ++	B -	B +	B ++	C -	C +	C ++	D -	D +	D ++
Cost		x			x				x	x		
Brand			x			x	x					x
Technology		x		x				x		x		
Employees	x				x		x				x	
Customer service		x				x			x		x	
Distribution			x	x				x		x		
Speed to market			x			x	x					x
Design		x		x			x				x	
Reliability		x		x					x			x

critical success factor

WHAT IS IT?

The critical success factor is the factor that is necessary for a project to achieve it's goal or mission. In order to be profitable and survive, a company needs to have a critical success factor.

WHO INVENTED IT?

The term success factor was developed by D. Ronald Daniel of McKinsey & Company in 1961. John F. Rockart further developed the concept of critical success factors between 1979 and 1981

WHY USE THIS METHOD?

1. It is a method of graphically representing a company's critical success factors so they can be the focus for discussion and refinement.
2. It is a method of comparing competitors

CHALLENGES

1. The method can be subjective

RESOURCES

1. Pen
2. Paper
3. Computer
4. Graphics software

WHEN TO USE THIS METHOD

1. Define intent

HOW TO USE THIS METHOD

1. Ask your team: 'Why would customers choose us?'."What do we need to do well to win business?" The answer is typically a critical success factor.
2. Create a matrix and rate each identified critical success factor an a 3 point scale.
3. Graph each score and connect the scores for each company being assessed with a line.

REFERENCES

1. Boynlon, A.C., and Zmud, R.W. 1984. "An Assessment of Critical Success Factors," Sloan Management Review (25:4), pp. 17-27.
2. Rockart, John F. "A Primer on Critical Success Factors" published in The Rise of Managerial Computing: The Best of the Center for Information Systems Research, edited with Christine V. Bullen. (Homewood, IL: Dow Jones-Irwin), 1981, OR, McGraw-Hill School Education Group (1986)
3. Johnson, James A. and Michael Friesen (1995). The Success Paradigm: Creating Organizational Effectiveness Through Quality and Strategy New York: Quorum Books. ISBN 978-0-89930-836-4

ANTICIPATE ENTER ENGAGE EXIT REVIEW

CUSTOMER MORE POSITIVE EXPERIENCES

CUSTOMER POSITIVE EXPERIENCES

BASELINE

CUSTOMER NEGATIVE EXPERIENCES

CUSTOMER MORE NEGATIVE EXPERIENCES

EMOTIONAL EXPERIENCE

customer experience map

WHAT IS IT?

Customer experience also called customer journey mapping is a method of documenting and visualizing the experiences that customers have as they use a product or service and their responses to their experiences.
It allows your team to access and analyze the interacting factors that form a customer experience.

WHY USE THIS METHOD?

1. Helps develop a consistent, predictable customer experience,
2. Presents an overview of your customer's experience from their point of view.
3. Helps reduce the number of dissatisfied customers
4. Can be used with different personas.

WHEN TO USE THIS METHOD

1. Know Context
2. Know User
3. Frame insights

HOW TO USE THIS METHOD

1. Identify your team.
2. Identify the customer experience to be analyzed. Identify the context. Identify personas.
3. Define the experience as a time line with stages such as anticipation, entry, engagement, exit, and reflection.
4. Use post-it notes to add positive and negative experiences to the relevant parts of the time line.
5. Order the experiences around a baseline by how positive or negative the experience were.
6. Analyze the parts of the time line and activities that have the most negative experiences. These are opportunities for design.

RESOURCES

1. Post-it-notes
2. Printed or projected template
3. White board
4. Markers

REFERENCES

1. Joshi, Hetal. "Customer Journey Mapping: The Road to Success." Cognizant. (2009) Web. 26 Jul. 2013.
2. World Class Skills Programme. "Customer Journey Mapping." Developing Responsive Provision. (2006): n. page. Web. 27 Jul. 2013.

DAY IN THE LIFE

After scanning the daily British newspapers, The Queen reviews her correspondence.

If there is an Investiture – a ceremony for the presentation of honours and decorations – it begins at 11.00am and lasts just over an hour

The Queen will often lunch privately. Every few months, she and The Duke of Edinburgh will invite a dozen guests from a wide variety of backgrounds to an informal lunch.

7 am 8 am 9 am 10 am 11 am 12 pm 1 pm 2 pm

Every day, 200–300 letters from the public arrive. The Queen chooses a selection to read herself and tells members of her staff how she would like them to be answered

A series of official meetings or 'audiences' will often follow. The Queen will see a number of important people.

In the afternoons, The Queen goes out on public engagements. The Queen prepares for each visit by briefing herself on whom she will be meeting and what she will be seeing and doing

day in the life

WHAT IS IT?

A study in which the designer observes the participant in the location and context of their usual activities, observing and recording events to understand the activities from the participant's point of view. This is sometimes repeated. Mapping a 'Day in the Life' as a storyboard can provide a focus for discussion.

WHO INVENTED IT?

ALex Bavelas 1944

WHY USE THIS METHOD?

1. This method informs the design process by observation of real activities and behaviors.
2. This method provides insights with relatively little cost and time.

CHALLENGES

1. Choose the participants carefully
2. Document everything. Something that seems insignificant may become significant later.

WHEN TO USE THIS METHOD

1. Know Context
2. Know User
3. Frame insights

HOW TO USE THIS METHOD

1. Define activities to study
2. Recruit participants
3. Prepare
4. Observe subjects in context.
5. Capture data.
6. Create storyboard with text and timeline.
7. Analyze data
8. Create insights.
9. Identify issues
10. Identify needs
11. Add new/more requirements to concept development

RESOURCES

1. Camera
2. Notebook
3. Video camera
4. Voice recorder
5. Pens

REFERENCES

1. Shadowing: And Other Techniques for Doing Fieldwork in Modern Societies [Paperback] Barbara Czarniawska. Publisher: Copenhagen Business School Pr (December 2007) ISBN-10: 8763002159 ISBN-13: 978-8763002158

DECISION RINGS

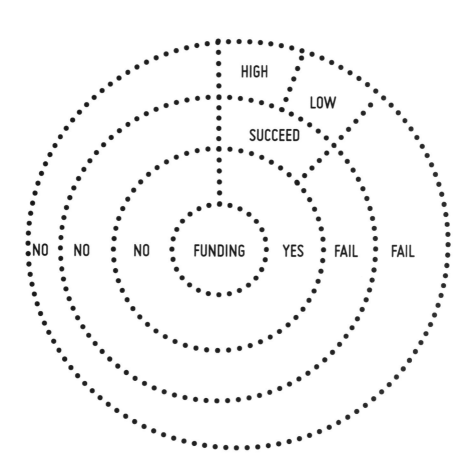

decision rings

WHAT IS IT?

Decision rings are a graphical way of visualizing the likelihood or benefit of the outcome of decisions.

WHY USE THIS METHOD?

1.   A visual way of representing a problem.

RESOURCES

1.   Pen
2.   Paper
3.   Computer
4.   Software

REFERENCES

1.   Tufte, E. (1992), The Visual Display of Quantitative Information, Graphics Press.
2.   Baron, J. & R. Brown (1991), Teaching Decisionmaking to Adolescents, Erlbaum.

WHEN TO USE THIS METHOD

1.   Define intent
2.   Frame insights
3.   Explore Concepts
4.   Make Plans

HOW TO USE THIS METHOD

1.   Draw a number of concentric circles.
2.   If your problem decision involves n stages, draw n+1 concentric circles.
3.   Split the first ring into segments equal to the number of choices for the first decision.
4.   Divide the next stage into segments based on the segments of the previous stage
5.   Divide each subsequent segment into the number of boxes equal to the alternative solutions.
6.   Divide each subsequent box into boxes proportional to the probability of the associated outcome
7.   Repeat for each decision stage.

DENDOGRAM

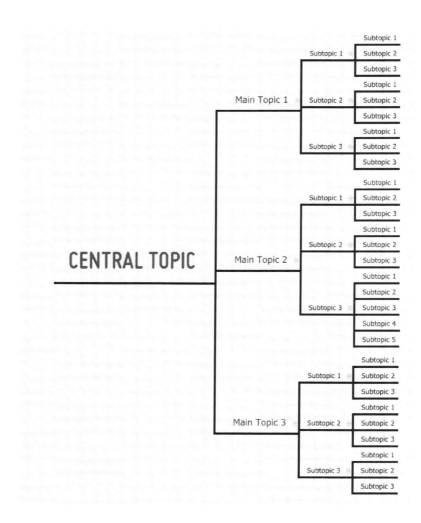

dendrogram

WHAT IS IT?

A dendrogram is a tree diagram used to illustrate hierarchical clustering. The distance of one group from the other groups indicates the degree of relationship

WHO INVENTED IT?

Carl Lamanna and M. Frank Mallette 1953

WHY USE THIS METHOD?

1. It is a visual method of displaying and communicating the relationship between a group of items or ideas.

WHEN TO USE THIS METHOD

1. Know Context
2. Know User
3. Frame insights

RESOURCES

1. Paper
2. Pen
3. White board
4. Dry-erase markers.

HOW TO USE THIS METHOD

1. Write down all of the items.
2. Determine how to cluster the items.
3. Name each group.
4. Connect the groups with lines.

Connect the larger groups and continue the process till the dendrogram is complete.

REFERENCES

1. Analyzing Animal Societies: Quantitative Methods for Vertebrate Social Analysis Hal Whitehead University of Chicago Press, Jul 15, 2008

EISENHOWER MAP

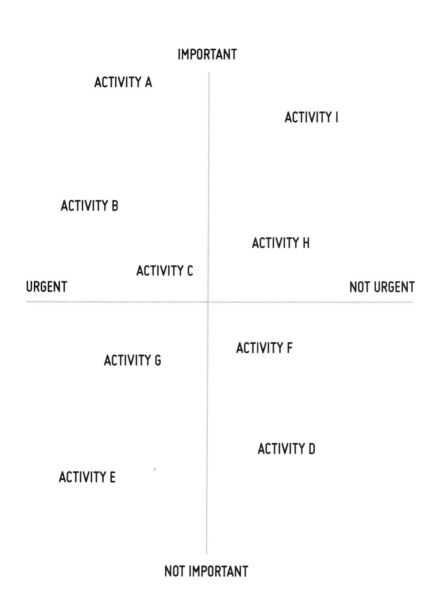

eisenhower map

WHAT IS IT?

The Eisenhower map is a simple tool that helps you manage your time effectively. also called "Eisenhower matrix", "Eisenhower principle", "Eisenhower grid" Eisenhower is quoted as saying, "What is important is seldom urgent and what is urgent is seldom important."

WHO INVENTED IT?

US President Dwight D. Eisenhower

WHY USE THIS METHOD?

1. Aids communication and discussion within the organization.
2. It is human nature to do tasks which are not most urgent first.
3. To gain competitive advantage,
4. Helps build competitive strategy
5. Helps build communication strategy
6. Helps manage time effectively

CHALLENGES

1. Can be subjective

WHEN TO USE THIS METHOD

1. Know Context
2. Know User
3. Frame insights
4. Explore Concepts

HOW TO USE THIS METHOD

1. Moderator draws grid on whiteboard or flip chart.
2. At the end of each project meeting the team brainstorms the tasks that need to be completed and places each task by consensus on the map.
3. Map individual tasks.
4. Interpret the map.
5. Create strategy.
6. Tasks which are important and urgent are given immediate resources.

RESOURCES

1. Pen
2. Paper
3. White board
4. Dry erase markers

EMOTIONAL JOURNEY MAP

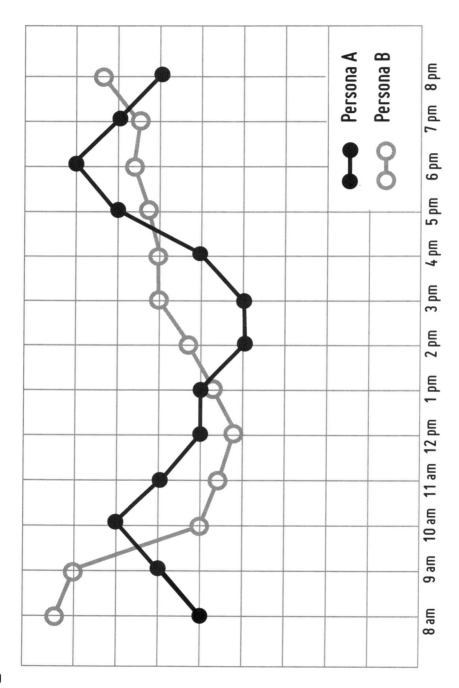

emotional journey map

WHAT IS IT?

An emotional journey map is a map that visually illustrates people's emotional experience throughout an interaction with an organization or brand.

WHY USE THIS METHOD?

1. It provides a focus for discussion
2. It focusses on what may make your customers unhappy
3. Provides a visually compelling story of customer experience. ,
4. Customer experience is more than interaction with a product.
5. By understanding the journey that your customers are making, you will be in a position to make informed improvements.

CHALLENGES

1. Customers often do not take the route in an interaction that the designer expects.
2. Failure to manage experiences can lead to lost customers.

WHEN TO USE THIS METHOD

1. Know Context
2. Know User
3. Frame insights
4. Explore Concepts
5. Make Plans

HOW TO USE THIS METHOD

1. Define the activity of your map. For example it could be a ride on the underground train.
2. Collect internal insights
3. Research customer perceptions
4. Analyze research
5. Map journey.
6. Across the top of the page do a time line Break the journey into stages using your customer's point of view
7. Capture each persona's unique experience
8. Use a scale from 0 to 10. The higher the number, the better the experience.
9. Plot the emotional journey.
10. Analyze the lease pleasant emotional periods and create ideas for improving the experience during those periods.
11. Create a map for each persona.

RESOURCES

1. Paper
2. Pens
3. White board
4. Post-it-notes

REFERENCES

1. Joshi, Hetal. "Customer Journey Mapping: The Road to Success." Cognizant. (2009) Web. 26 Jul. 2013.
2. World Class Skills Programme. "Customer Journey Mapping." Developing Responsive Provision. (2006): n. page. Web. 27 Jul. 2013.

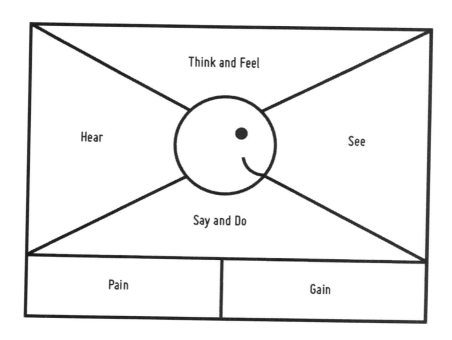

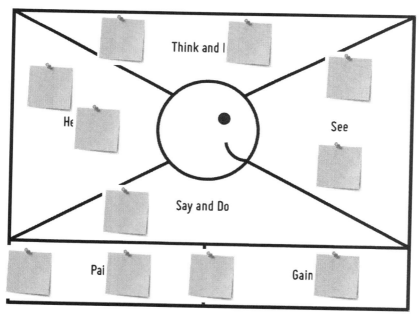

empathy map

WHAT IS IT?
Empathy Map is a tool that helps the design team empathize with people they are designing for, You can create an empathy map for a group of customers or a persona.

WHO INVENTED IT?
Scott Matthews and Dave Gray at PLANE now Dachis Group.

WHY USE THIS METHOD?
This tool helps a design team understand the customers and their context.

CHALLENGES
1. Emotions must be inferred by observing clues.
2. This method does not provide the same level of rigor as traditional personas but requires less investment.

WHEN TO USE THIS METHOD
1. Know Context
2. Know User
3. Frame insights

RESOURCES
1. Empathy map template
2. White board
3. Dry-erase markers
4. Post-it-notes
5. Pens
6. Video Camera

HOW TO USE THIS METHOD
1. A team of 3 to 10 people is a good number for this method.
2. This method can be used with personas.
3. Draw a cirle to represent your target persona.
4. Divide the circle into sections that represent aspects of that person's sensory experience.
5. Ask your team to describe from the persona's point of view their experience.
6. What are the persona's needs and desires?
7. Populate the map by taking note of the following traits of your user as you review your notes, audio, and video from your fieldwork: What are they thinking, feeling, saying, doing, hearing, seeing?
8. Fill in the diagram with real, tangible, sensory experiences.
9. 20 minutes to one hour is a good duration for this exercise.
10. Ask another group of people to look at your map and suggest improvements or refinements.

REFERENCES
1. Gray, Dave; Brown, Sunni; Macanufo, James (2010). Gamestorming: A Playbook for Innovators, Rulebreakers, and Changemakers. O'Reilly Media, Inc

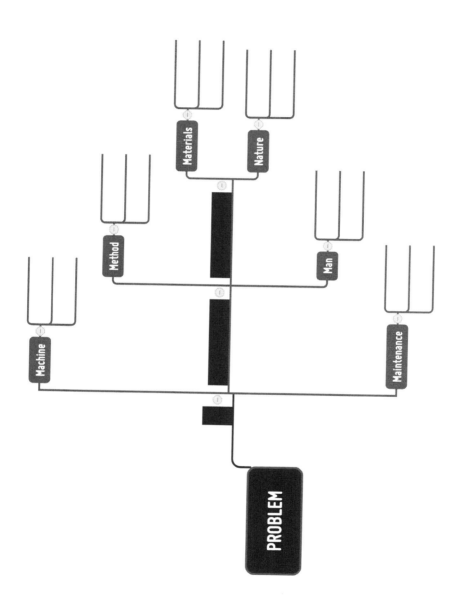

fishbone diagram

WHAT IS IT?

Fishbone diagrams also called Ishikawa diagrams, are diagrams that show the causes of a specific event.

Mazda Motors used an Ishikawa diagram to design the Miata sports car, The goal was was "Jinba Ittai" Horse and Rider as One. Every factor identified in the diagram was included in the final design. Ishikawa described the process as fishboning your problem and letting it cook overnight.

WHO INVENTED IT?

Kaoru Ishikawa University of Tokyo 1968

WHY USE THIS METHOD?

1. People tend to fix a problem by responding to an immediately visible cause while ignoring the deeper issues. This approach may lead to a problem reoccurring.
2. Use in the predesign phase to understand the root causes of a problem to serve as the basis for design.
3. Identifies the relationship between cause and effect.

WHEN TO USE THIS METHOD

1. Define intent
2. Know Context
3. Know User
4. Frame insights

HOW TO USE THIS METHOD

1. Prepare the six arms of the Ishikawa Diagram on a white board.
2. Define the problem clearly as a short statement in the head of the diagram.
3. Describe the causes of each bone and write them at the end of each branch. Use the 4 M's as categories; Machine, Man Methods, Materials.
4. Conduct the brainstorming session using brainstorming guidelines Ask each team member to define the cause of the problem. You may list as many causes as necessary. Typically 3 to 6 are listed.
5. Minor causes are then listed around the major causes.
6. Interpret the Ishikawa Diagram once it's finished.

RESOURCES

1. White board
2. Dry-erase markers
3. Room with privacy
4. Paper
5. Pens

REFERENCES

1. Ishikawa, Kaoru, Guide to Quality Control, Asian Productivity Organization, UNIPUB, 1976, ISBN 92-833-1036-5
2. Ishikawa, Kaoru (1990); (Translator: J. H. Loftus); Introduction to Quality Control; 448 p; ISBN 4-906224-61-X OCLC 41428

FORCE FIELD DIAGRAM

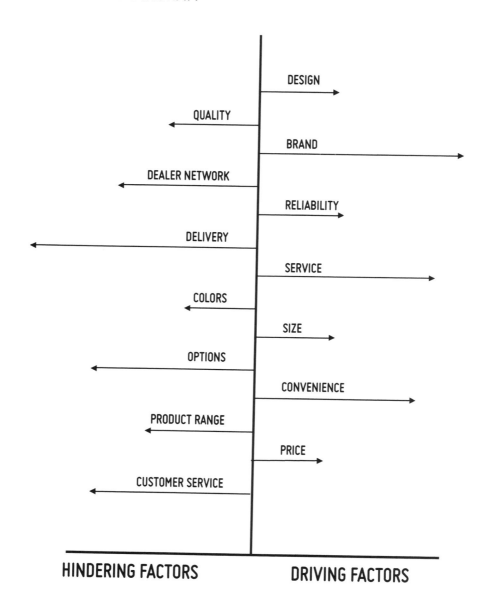

HINDERING FACTORS   DRIVING FACTORS

force field analysis

WHAT IS IT?
Force field analysis is a method of mapping and analyzing factors which assist or work against desired goals.

WHO INVENTED IT?
Kurt Lewin 1940s
John R. P. French 1947

WHY USE THIS METHOD?
1. Allows visual comparison of factors affecting the success of a project for discussion of solutions.

CHALLENGES
1. It is best to focus on barriers.
2. Assign a strategy to each barrier

RESOURCES
1. Pen
2. Paper
3. White board
4. Dry erase markers
5. Post-it notes.

REFERENCES
1. Cartwright, D. (1951). Foreword to the 1951 Edition. Field Theory in Social Science and Selected Theoretical Papers– Kurt Lewin. Washington, D.C.: American Psychological Association, 1997. Originally published by Harper & Row.

WHEN TO USE THIS METHOD
1. Define intent
2. Know Context
3. Know User

HOW TO USE THIS METHOD
1. Select a moderator and a team of stakeholders.
2. The moderator describes the problem being focused on to the team
3. The moderator draws the letter T on a white board
4. The moderator writes the problem above the cross stroke on the T
5. The team brainstorms a list of forces working against the goal and the moderator lists them on the right hand of the upstroke on the letter T.
6. The team brainstorms a list or forces working towards the goal and the moderator writes them on the right hand of the upstroke on the letter T.
7. Forces listed can be internal and external.
8. They can be associated with the environment, the organization, people strategy, culture, values, competitors, conflicts or other factors.
9. Prioritize and quantify both lists of forces
10. The moderator draws a horizontal letter T and above the horizontal line draws arrows for each factor indicating their relative significance in the opinion of the team.
11. The moderator draws arrows for each negative factor below the line showing their relative significance.

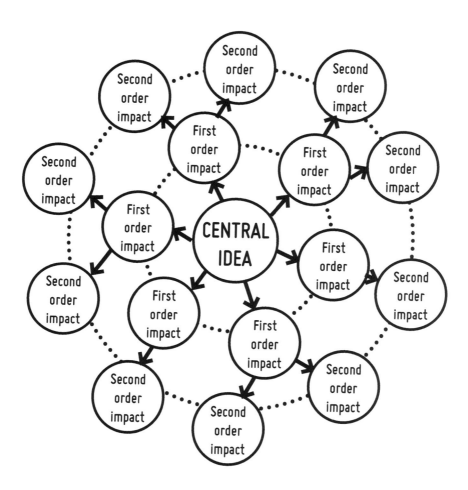

future wheel

WHAT IS IT?
The future wheel is a method to graphically represent and analyze the direct and indirect outcomes of a proposed change.

WHO INVENTED IT?
Jerome Glenn 1972

WHY USE THIS METHOD?
1. A method of envisioning outcomes of decisions.
2. Can be used to study possible outcomes of trends.
3. Helps create a consciousness of the future.

CHALLENGES
1. Can be subjective

WHEN TO USE THIS METHOD
1. Define intent

HOW TO USE THIS METHOD
1. Define the proposed change
2. Identify and graph the first level of outcomes
3. Identify and graph the subsequent level of outcomes
4. Link the dependencies
5. Identify insights
6. Identify the actions
7. Implement the actions

RESOURCES
1. Pen
2. Paper
3. White board
4. Dry erase markers

REFERENCES
1. Futures Wheel, Futures Research Methodology Version 3.0, The Millennium Project, Washington, DC 2009

gantt chart

WHAT IS IT?

A Gantt chart is a bar chart that shows the tasks of a project, the start time and the time from start to completion of each task.

This method is used widely in industry to ensure that activities are completed on time and on budget.

WHO INVENTED IT?

Henry Gantt first published in "Organizing for Work 1919.

WHY USE THIS METHOD?

1. Use to track a design project
2. Use to ensure that tasks are completed on time.

WHEN TO USE THIS METHOD

1. Define intent
2. Know Context
3. Know User
4. Frame insights
5. Explore Concepts
6. Make Plans
7. Deliver Offering

RESOURCES

1. Pen
2. Paper
3. Gantt Chart software

HOW TO USE THIS METHOD

1. Identify the tasks
2. Identify the milestones in the project.
3. Identify the time required for each task.
4. Identify the order and dependencies of each task.
5. Identify the tasks that can be undertaken in parallel
6. Draw a horizontal time axis along the top or bottom of a page.
7. Draw a list of tasks in order down the left hand side of the page in the order that they should be undertaken.
8. Draw a diamond for tasks that are short in duration such as a meeting
9. For longer activities draw a horizontal bar indicating the planned duration.

REFERENCES

1. Gantt, Henry L., A graphical daily balance in manufacture, Transactions of the American Society of Mechanical Engineers, VolumeXIV, pages 1322—1336, 1903.
2. Gerard Blokdijk, Project Management 100 Success Secrets, Lulu.com, 2007

GOAL GRID

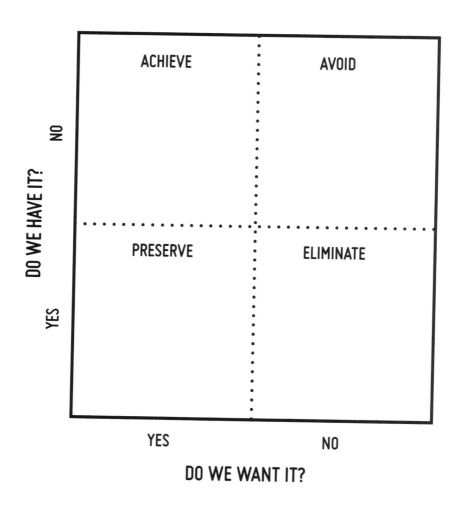

goal grid

WHAT IS IT?
A goal grid is a method for clarifying goals.

"The Goals Grid also provides a structure for analyzing patterns in goals and objectives and for detecting potential conflict with the goals and objectives of others." *Fred Nickols*

WHO INVENTED IT?
Ray Forbes, John Arnold and Fred Nickols 1992

WHY USE THIS METHOD?
1. A goal grid is a method for clarifying goals.

RESOURCES
1. Pen
2. Paper
3. White board
4. Dry erase markers
5. Post-it notes.

WHEN TO USE THIS METHOD
1. Define intent

HOW TO USE THIS METHOD
1. The team brainstorms a list of goals.
2. The moderator asks the team these questions:
   ◦ "Do we have it?"
   ◦ "Do we want it?"
   ◦ "What are we trying to achieve?"
   ◦ "What are we trying to preserve?"
   ◦ "What are we trying to avoid?"
   ◦ "What are we trying to eliminate?"

REFERENCES
1. Arnold, John D. (1980). The Art of Decision Making. AMACOM, New York.
2. Barnard, Chester A (1938). The Functions of the Executive. Harvard University Press, Cambridge
3. Nickols, Fred (2003) The Goals Grid: A Tool for Clarifying Goals & Objectives

GOZINTO CHART

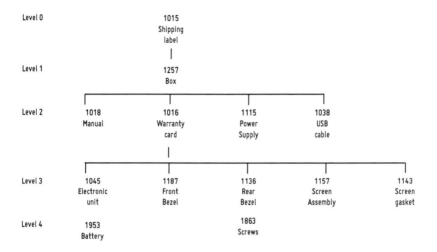

Level 0   1015
Shipping
label

Level 1   1257
Box

Level 2   1018   1016   1115   1038
Manual   Warranty   Power   USB
card   Supply   cable

Level 3   1045   1187   1136   1157   1143
Electronic   Front   Rear   Screen   Screen
unit   Bezel   Bezel   Assembly   gasket

Level 4   1953   1863
Battery   Screws

gozinto chart

WHAT IS IT?

The Gozinto chart is a type of tree diagram that shows levels of an assembly. It is a tree representation of a product that shows how the elements required to assemble a product fit together. Gozinto is derived from the phrase "What goes into it?"

WHO INVENTED IT?

A. Vazsonyi

WHY USE THIS METHOD?

1. To breakdown a product into its parts.
2. To illustrate the assembly process.
3. To cross-reference parts data with the hierarchical levels of assembly.

CHALLENGES

1. Gozinto chart numbering is by levels and bill of materials or parts list number.

WHEN TO USE THIS METHOD

1. Know Context
2. Know User
3. Frame insights

HOW TO USE THIS METHOD

1. Create a list of all the parts of a product or a system
2. Draw a hierarchy of assembly
3. Provide identification of parts; name and number each part charted.
4. Review and refine

RESOURCES

1. Pen
2. Paper
3. White board
4. Dry erase markers

HEPTALYSIS

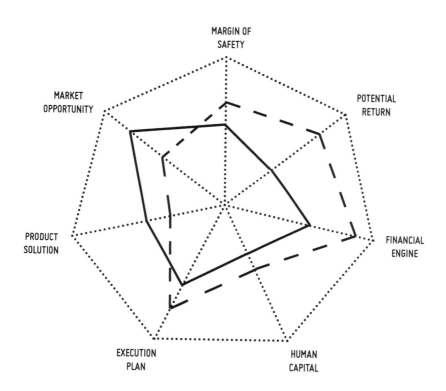

heptalysis

WHAT IS IT?

Heptalysis is a method used to perform an in-depth analysis of early stage businesses ventures using seven criteria for evaluation.

The criteria are:

1. Margin of safety
2. Potential return
3. Financial engine
4. Human capital
5. Execution plan
6. Product solution
7. Market opportunity

WHY USE THIS METHOD?

1. Used for analyzing a new product idea for raising venture capital
2. Use for analyzing what resources are necessary
3. Use for understanding risk.

WHEN TO USE THIS METHOD

1. Define intent
2. Know Context
3. Know User

RESOURCES

1. Pen
2. Paper
3. White board
4. Dry erase markers
5. Post-it notes

HOW TO USE THIS METHOD

Market Opportunity.

1. Who are the potential customers for this product?
2. What is the benefit of it for the customers?
3. Where and how it can be used?
4. What is our advantage over the competitors who produce the same product?
5. Is there a sustainable market for the product?
6. When is the best time to introduce the product to the market

Source Finance NZ, http://financenz.wordpress. com/ (accessed December 28, 2013).

Product/Solution.

1. What are we going to bring to market, service, product or a combination of them?
2. Are there any follow-up products?
3. Are the follow-up products in the scope of our activity?

Execution Plan.

1. Marketing and Promotion
2. Sales and Distribution
3. Production and Quality
4. Compensation
5. Growth
6. Potential Return.
7. What is the expected share of market?
8. What is the pricing strategy?
9. Is the price affordable by the majority of potential customers?
10. How long does it take to achieve profits?

Source: Deepan Siddhu

Infographic elements

Statistics

Lorem ipsum dolor sit amet, consectetur adipiscing elit. Phasellus laoreet rhoncus massa, rhoncus consequat enim tempor at.

Lorem ipsum dolor sit amet, consectetur adipiscing elit. Phasellus laoreet rhoncus massa, rhoncus consequat enim tempor at. Nunc ultricies varius sollicitudin. In id ullamcorper leo.

75%   **67%**   **69%**   **75%**

Lorem ipsum dolor sit amet
Consectetur adipiscing elit
Phasellus laoreet
Lorem ipsum
rhoncus consequat
Nunc ultricies sollicitudin
enim ullamcorper leo

Human Resources

Energy Used

Lorem ipsum dolor sit amet, consectetur adipiscing elit. Phasellus laoreet rhoncus massa, rhoncus consequat enim tempor at.

Lorem ipsum dolor sit amet, consectetur adipiscing elit. Phasellus laoreet rhoncus massa, rhoncus consequat enim tempor at. Nunc ultricies varius sollicitudin. In id ullamcorper leo.

50% **60%** **54%** **67%** **75%**

2011 2012 2013 2014 2015

Analytics

40 30 20 10 0

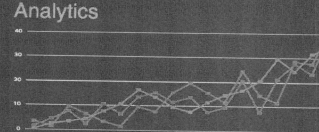

Donec volutpat, lacus id dignissim dictum, ante quam semper puru nec scelerisque ligula arcu in mi. Nullam eget tempus dolor.

WAR

Lorem ipsum dolor sit amet, consectetur adipiscing elit. Phasellus laoreet rhoncus massa, rhoncus consequat enim tempor at.

PEACE

Lorem ipsum dolor sit amet, consectetur adipiscing elit. Phasellus laoreet rhoncus massa, rhoncus consequat enim tempor at.

Statistics (drinks)

Lorem ipsum dolor sit amet, consectetur adipiscing elit. Phasellus laoreet rhoncus massa, rhoncus consequat enim tempor at. Nunc ultricies varius sollicitudin. In id ullamcorper leo.

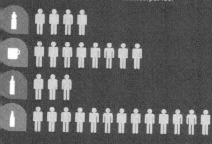

2011 2012

67%
75%
80%

Media Stats

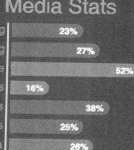

Department blog — 23%
Personal blog — 27%
Company website — 52%
Podcasts — 16%
Overviews — 38%
Journals — 25%
Social media — 26%
Newspapers — 17%

Appreciated:

55%   7%   38%

Lorem ipsum dolor sit amet, consectetur adipiscing elit. Phasellus laoreet rhoncus massa, rhoncus consequat enim tempor at.

infographic

WHAT IS IT?
An infographic is a graphic that displays information. The aim of an infographic is to present complex information and clearly communicate the significance of the data.

WHO INVENTED IT?
Some prehistoric cave paintings may have functioned as infographics.

WHY USE THIS METHOD?
1. Use infographics to communicate complex information

WHEN TO USE THIS METHOD
1. Frame insights

RESOURCES
1. Infographic vector elements
2. Computer graphics software
3. Computer

REFERENCES
1. John Emerson (2008). Visualizing Information for Advocacy: An Introduction to Information Design. New York: OSI.
2. Sandra Rendgen, Julius Wiedemann (2013). Information Graphics. Taschen Publishing. ISBN 978-3836528795

johari's window

WHAT IS IT?

The Johari window is a method of understanding relationships between people. Helps us understand how others see us and how we see ourselves. It helps communicate information about people and perceptions.

WHO INVENTED IT?

Joseph Luft and Harry Ingham 1955 combining their first names, Joe and Harry.

WHY USE THIS METHOD?

1. The Johari window is a way of representing information about people feelings, experiences, attitudes, skills,and motivation, from four perspectives.
2. Helps identify what are the gaps in knowledge and where further research needs to be undertaken.

WHEN TO USE THIS METHOD

1. Know Context
2. Know User
3. Frame insights

RESOURCES

1. Paper
2. Pens
3. White board
4. Dry erase markers

HOW TO USE THIS METHOD

1. Open: The team and participants select adjectives to place in this quadrant that describe the traits of the subjects that both are aware of.
2. Hidden: Adjectives are selected by subjects to describe the traits that the team are not aware of.
3. Blind Spot: These adjectives are selected by the team to describe things that the subjects are not aware of but others are.
4. Unknown: These are adjectives not selected by either the team or the subjects in other quadrants.

REFERENCES

1. Hase, Steward; Alan Davies, Bob Dick (1999). The Johari Window and the Dark Side of Organizations. Southern Cross University.

JOHARI'S WINDOW

NOT KNOWN TO SELF

KNOWN TO OTHERS

ARENA | BLIND SPOT

FACADE | UNKNOWN

NOT KNOWN TO OTHERS

johari's window

ADJECTIVES

able
accepting
adaptable
bold
brave
calm
caring
cheerful
clever
complex
confident
dependable
dignified
Energetic
extroverted
friendly
giving
happy
helpful
idealistic
independent
ingenious
intelligent
introverted
kind
knowledgeable
logical
loving

mature
modest
nervous
observant
organized
patient
powerful
proud
quiet
reflective
relaxed
religious
responsive
searching
self-assertive
self-conscious
sensible
sentimental
shy
silly
smart
spontaneous
sympathetic
tense
trustworthy
warm
wise
witty

KANO ANALYSIS

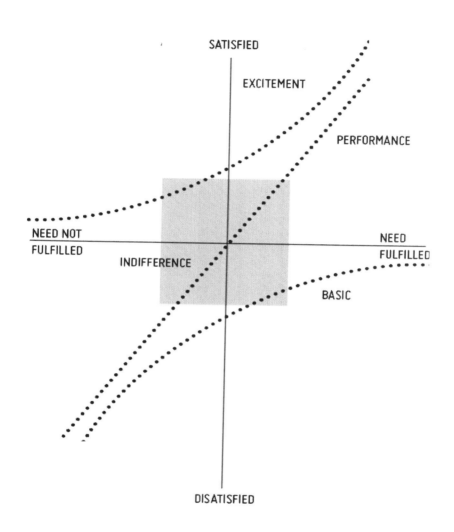

kano analysis

WHAT IS IT?
The Kano model of customer satisfaction clas-
sifies product attributes based on customer
perception and satisfaction.

WHO INVENTED IT?
Dr Noriaki Kano 1980s

WHY USE THIS METHOD?
Strategically guides design decisions
Identifies customer needs
Determines functional requirements
Useful for concept development
Analyzing competitive products

CHALLENGES
1. Shouldn't be applied after the design is
    complete
2. Prioritization matrices help in under-
    standing what excites the customer.

WHEN TO USE THIS METHOD
3. Know Context
4. Know User
5. Frame insights
6. Explore Concepts

HOW TO USE THIS METHOD
Ask customers:
1. Rate your satisfaction with this
    attribute?
2. Rate your satisfaction without this
    attribute?

Customers should select one of the following
responses:
1. Satisfied;
2. Neutral (Its normally that way);
3. Dissatisfied;
4. Don't care.

REFERENCES
1. Kano, Noriaki; Nobuhiku Seraku, Fumio
    Takahashi, Shinichi Tsuji (April 1984).
    "Attractive quality and must-be quality"
    (in Japanese). Journal of the Japanese
    Society for Quality Control 14 (2):
    39—48. ISSN 0386-8230.
2. Bartikowski, B., Llosa, S. (2003).
    Identifying Satisfiers, Dissatisfiers,
    Criticals and Neutrals in Customer
    Satisfaction. Working Paper n° 05-
    2003, Mai 2003. Euromed – Ecole de
    Management. Marseille.

LINE CHART

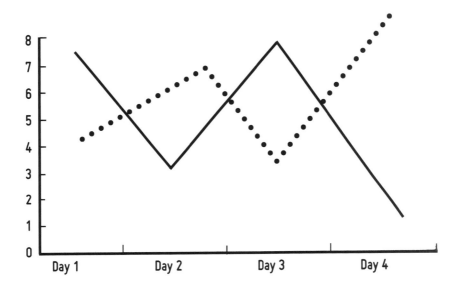

●●●●●●●● Designers working on project in Beijing

───────── Designers working on project in London

line chart

WHAT IS IT?
A line chart is a type of chart that is often used to show trends over time

WHY USE THIS METHOD?
1. To display tends over time.

RESOURCES
1. Pen
2. Paper
3. White board
4. Dry erase markers

REFERENCES
1. Neil J. Salkind (2006). Statistics for People who (think They) Hate Statistics: The Excel Edition. page 106.

WHEN TO USE THIS METHOD
1. Frame insights

HOW TO USE THIS METHOD
1. Collect data
2. The horizontal axis is called the X axis and the vertical axis is called the Y axis
3. Draw an X and a Y axis.
4. The Y axis is typically the time intervals such as years or months.
5. Select suitable scales
6. Plot the data points
7. Join the data pints with lines.
8. Add the title and a legend or key if required.

LINKING DIAGRAM

Objectives	Weighting	Responsibility

Reduce SKUs by 25% — 10 — Industrial Design

Engineering

Establish new factory in China — 8 — Transportation

Decrease returns by 25% — 6 — Human Resources

Manufacturing

Increase sales by 25% — 7 — Quality

Establish distribution Network in China — 7 — Marketing

Sales

Increase speed to market by 30% — 4 — Sourcing

Reduce manufacturing costs by 25% — 9 — Management

linking diagram

WHAT IS IT?
A linking diagram is a graphical method of displaying relationships between factors in data sets.

WHY USE THIS METHOD?
1. To analyze relationships of complex data

RESOURCES
1. Pen
2. Paper
3. White board
4. Dry erase markers

WHEN TO USE THIS METHOD
1. Know Context
2. Know User
3. Frame insights

HOW TO USE THIS METHOD
1. Select a problem to analyze.
2. Team brainstorms two lists of factors that relate to the problem such as outcomes and actions.
3. Team rates the items by importance. 1–10, 10 being most important.
4. Draw lines between related items in each list.
5. Review and refine
6. List insights
7. Take actions based on the insights.

market segmentation

WHAT IS IT?

A market segment is a group of people with characteristics in common. A market segment is distinct from other segments, it exhibits common needs; it responds similarly to a market stimulus, and it can be reached by a market intervention.

WHO INVENTED IT?

Wendel Smith 1956

WHY USE THIS METHOD?

1. The purpose for segmenting a market is to allow you to focus on people that are "most likely" to use your design.
2. This will help optimize your return on investment.

CHALLENGES

1. Everyone is different.
2. Market segmentation assumes uniformity.
3. Internet based techniques will allow marketing to be done on a customized individual basis.

WHEN TO USE THIS METHOD

1. Know Context
2. Know User
3. Frame insights
4. Generate Concepts
5. Create Solutions

HOW TO USE THIS METHOD

1. Based on what people do
Use and behavior, activities or interests
2. Based on who people are
3. Based on how people think or feel
Attitudes,Needs behaviors and motivations
4. A combination of factors

REFERENCES

1. What is geographic segmentation' Kotler, Philip, and Kevin Lane Keller. Marketing Management. Prentice Hall, 2006. ISBN 978-0-13-145757-7
2. Goldstein, Doug. "What is Customer Segmentation?" Mind of Marketing.net, May 2007. New York, NY.
3. Sheth-Voss, Pieter. Carreras, Ismael. How Informative is Your Segmentation? A simple new metric yields surprising results, Marketing Research, pages 8-13, Winter 2010, American Marketing Association

MIND MAP

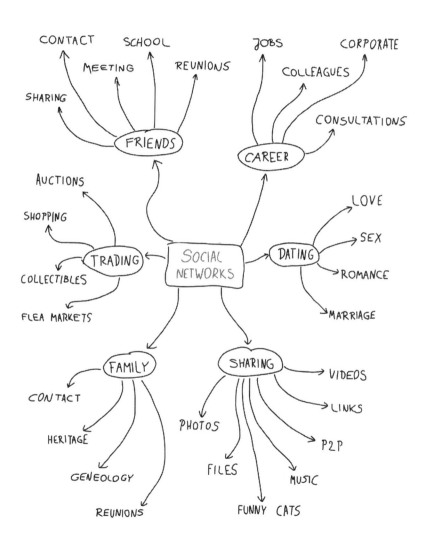

mind map

WHAT IS IT?

A mind map is a diagram used to represent the affinities or connections between a number of ideas or things. Understanding connections is the starting point for design. Mind maps are a method of analyzing information and relationships.

WHO INVENTED IT?

Porphry of Tyros 3rd century BC.
Allan Collins, Northwestern University 1960, USA

WHY USE THIS METHOD?

1. The method helps identify relationships.
2. There is no right or wrong with mind maps. They help with they help with memory and organization.
3. Problem solving and brainstorming
4. Relationship discovery
5. Summarizing information
6. Memorizing information

CHALLENGES

Print words clearly, use color and images for visual impact.

WHEN TO USE THIS METHOD

7. Know Context
8. Know User
9. Frame insights
10. Explore Concepts
11. Make Plans

HOW TO USE THIS METHOD

1. Start in the center with a key word or idea. Put box around this node.
2. Use images, symbols, or words for nodes.
3. Select key words.
4. Keep the key word names of nodes s simple and short as possible.
5. Associated nodes should be connected with lines to show affinities.
6. Make the lines the same length as the word/image they support.
7. Use emphasis such as thicker lines to show the strength of associations in your mind map.
8. Use radial arrangement of nodes.

RESOURCES

1. Paper
2. Pens
3. White board
4. Dry-erase markers

REFERENCES

1. Mind maps as active learning tools', by Willis, CL. Journal of computing sciences in colleges. ISSN: 1937-4771. 2006. Volume: 21 Issue: 4
2. Mind Maps as Classroom Exercises John W. Budd The Journal of Economic Education, Vol. 35, No. 1 (Winter, 2004), pp. 35-46 Published by: Taylor & Francis, Ltd.

mood board

WHAT IS IT?

A mood board is a collage made of images and words and may include sample of colors and fabrics or other materials. They are used to convey the emotional communication of an intended design

WHO INVENTED IT?

Possibly Terence Conran 1991

WHY USE THIS METHOD?

1. A mood board helps convey complex emotional ideas at an early stage in design project
2. Provides a focus for team discussion and alignment.
3. It is fast
4. Inexpensive
5. A form of visual prototype of a perceptual experience

CHALLENGES

1. It is subjective,

WHEN TO USE THIS METHOD

1. Define intent

HOW TO USE THIS METHOD

A mood board can include

1. Colors
2. Forms
3. Cultures
4. Materials
5. Finishes
6. Textures

RESOURCES

1. Graphic programs
2. Print Magazines
3. Digital images
4. Fabric swatches
5. Color swatches
6. Graphics software
7. Computer

REFERENCES

1. Kathryn McKelvey, Janine Munslow Fashion Forecasting :Page 150 2008
2. Product Design: Practical Methods for systematic Development of New Products By Mike Baxter 1995

network map

WHAT IS IT?
This is a method which maps and helps the researcher understand systems or services that involve many stakeholders. The map identifies the stakeholders, their links, influence and goals.

WHO INVENTED IT?
Eva Schiffer 2004 to 2008

WHY USE THIS METHOD?
1. Inexpensive and fast.
2. Connects to existing research tools and methods
3. Makes implicit knowledge explicit
4. Structures complex reality
5. Flexible for use in different contexts.

RESOURCES
1. Large sheets of paper for network map
2. Felt pens for drawing links
3. Adhesive paper as actor cards
4. Flat discs for building Influence-towers
5. Actor figurines

SEE ALSO
1. Actors map

WHEN TO USE THIS METHOD
1. Know Context
2. Know User
3. Frame insights

HOW TO USE THIS METHOD
1. Define problems and goals.
2. Recruit participants
3. Define interview questions
4. Define network links to study
5. Ask participant to go through the process in detail.
6. Make a card with the name and description of each stakeholder. Place the cards on your map.
7. Show links between the stakeholders as lines on the map.
8. Number the links.
9. Create a legend describing each link.
10. Setting up influence towers:
11. Describe the influence of each stakeholder.?
12. Quantify the strength of influence of each stakeholder.
13. Stack discs next to each stakeholder card showing the relative level of influence.
14. Write descriptions of perceived problems next to each stakeholder.

REFERENCES
1. Eva Schiffer http://netmap.wordpress.com/process-net-map

INTERVIEW PROCESS

Question 1: Who is involved?

Ask: "Who is involved in this process?"Write names on actor cards (with different colors of cards for different groups of actors) and distribute on empty Net-Map sheet.

Question 2: How are they linked?

Ask: "Who is linked to whom?" Go through the different kinds of links one by one Draw arrows between actor cards according to interviewee directions. If two actors exchange something draw double headed arrows. If actors exchange more than one thing, add differently colored arrow heads to existing links.

Question 3: How influential are they?

Ask: "How strongly can actors influence (our complex issue)?" Explain / agree on a definition of influence with your interviewee, clarify that this is about influence only and not influence in the world at large. Ask interviewee to assign influence towers to actors: The higher the influence on the issue at stake, the higher the tower. Towers of different actors can be of the same height. Actors with no influence can be put on ground level. Towers can be as high as participants want. Place influence towers next to actor cards. Verbalize set-up and give interviewee the chance to adjust towers before noting height of tower on the Net-Map.

Question 4: What are their goals?

Ask according to pre-defined goals, actor by actor, e.g. "Does this actor support environmental, developmental goals or both?" Note abbreviations for goals next to actor cards, allow for multiple goals where appropriate, by noting more than one goal next to the actor.

Discussion

Discuss the result with your interview partners. Depending on the goal of this specific mapping process, you might ask your participants to think strategically about the network and develop ideas to improve the situation in the future.

Source: Eva Schiffer http://netmap.wordpress.com/process-net-map

OBJECTIVES TREE

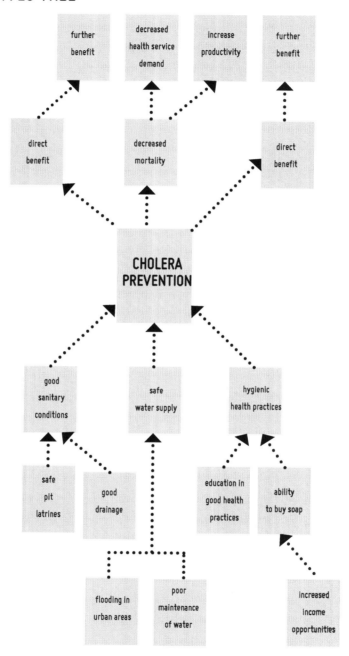

Source: Adapted from Water Supply and Sanitation Collaborative Council

objectives tree

WHAT IS IT?

You can convert your problem tree into a solution tree to define your goals and objectives. Rephrase each of the problems into positive desirable outcomes — as if the problem has already been treated.

CHALLENGES

1. Consider the likely stakeholders and constraints.

WHEN TO USE THIS METHOD

1. Define intent

SEE ALSO

1. Problem Tree

HOW TO USE THIS METHOD

1. Write your goal, a reversal of your particular problem, in the center of a large flip chart (trunk).
2. Write the benefits that will accrue if this goal is achieved (branches and leaves).
3. Write the steps or actions you need to take to achieve that goal (primary and secondary roots).

Source: Adapted from Water Supply and Sanitation Collaborative Council

RESOURCES

1. Pen
2. Paper
3. White board

ONION MAP

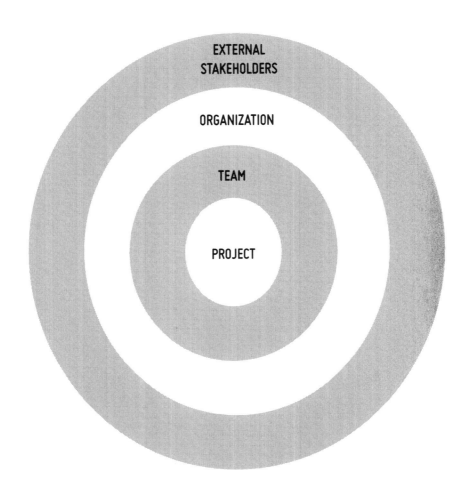

onion map

WHAT IS IT?
An onion map is a chart that shows dependencies of a system. The items in each circle depend on the items in the smaller circle.

WHO INVENTED IT?
Onion models have been used for centuries to indicate hierarchical levels of dependency. Peter Apian's 1539 Cosmographia used an onion model to illustrate the pre-Copernican model of the universe.

WHY USE THIS METHOD?
1. It is an effective way of describing complex relationships
2. It provides a focus for team discussion and alignment
3. It is fast
4. It is inexpensive.

WHEN TO USE THIS METHOD
1. Know Context
2. Know User
3. Frame insights

HOW TO USE THIS METHOD
1. Define the system to be represented by the onion diagram.
2. Create a circle to define the innermost level of dependency
3. Create concentric circles around the inner circle to represent progressively higher levels of dependency
4. Name the levels.

RESOURCES
1. Pen
2. Paper
3. Software
4. Computer
5. White board
6. Dry-erase markers

REFERENCES
1. Hofstede, G. (1992). Culture and Organisations: Software of the Mind. McGraw Hill, Maidenhead

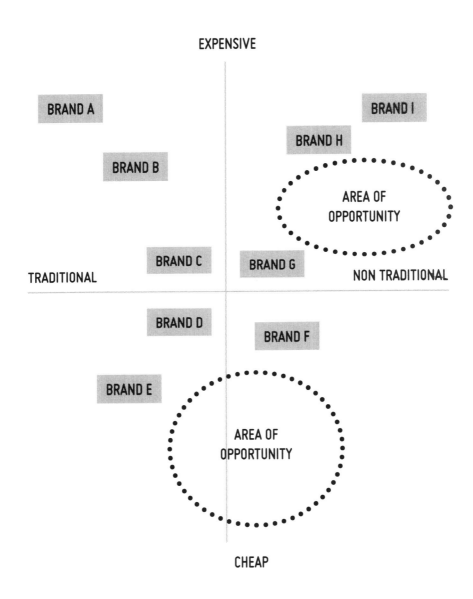

perceptual map

WHAT IS IT?

Perceptual mapping is a method that creates a map of the perceptions of people of competing alternatives to be compared.

WHO INVENTED IT?

Unknown

WHY USE THIS METHOD?

1. Aids communication and discussion within the organization
2. To gain competitive advantage,
3. Helps build competitive strategy
4. Helps build communication strategy
5. Helps identify potential new products
6. Helps build brand strategy

CHALLENGES

1. Because the position of a product or service on the map is subjective, you can ask several people to locate the position through group discussion.
2. Works well for clearly defined functional attributes such as price, product features

WHEN TO USE THIS METHOD

1. Know Context
2. Know User
3. Frame insights
4. Explore Concepts

HOW TO USE THIS METHOD

1. Define characteristics of product or service to map.
2. Identify competing brands, services or products to map.
3. Map individual items.
4. Interpret the map.
5. Create strategy.

RESOURCES

1. Pen
2. Paper
3. White board
4. Dry erase markers

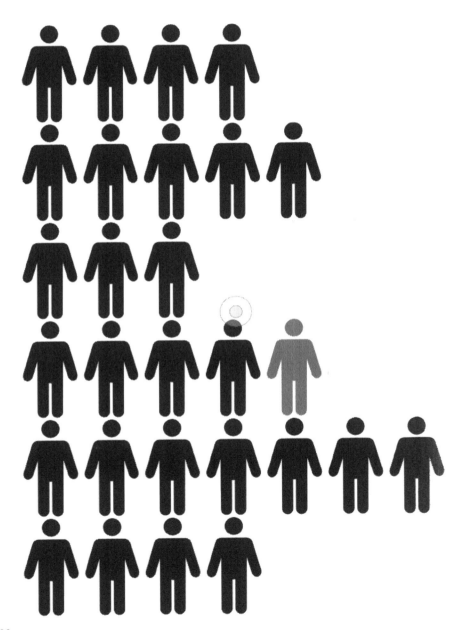

pictogram

WHAT IS IT?

A pictograph is a visual representation of a word or idea. A pictogram conveys it's meaning through it's resemblance to a physical object

WHO INVENTED IT?

Used since ancient times.
George Dow 1936

WHY USE THIS METHOD?

1. Conveys information in an understandable and visual way.
2. Does not require written language to convey meaning.
3. Used where it is necessary to understand the meaning fast such as emergency exits.

WHEN TO USE THIS METHOD

4. Know Context
5. Know User
6. Frame insights

RESOURCES

1. Pen
2. Paper
3. Computer
4. Graphic software

HOW TO USE THIS METHOD

1. Collect data
1. Construct or select suitable pictogram symbol.
1. Plot the data to visually represent the quantity of items.
1. Review and refine

REFERENCES

1. Modley, R. 1976 Handbook of Pictorial Symbols: 3, 250 Examples from International Sources
2. Chambers M. 2004 'Creating icons that really work', in Computer Arts June pp. 38-43
3. Gove, Philip Babcock. (1993). Webster's Third New International Dictionary of the English Language Unabridged. Merriam-Webster Inc. ISBN 0-87779-201-1.

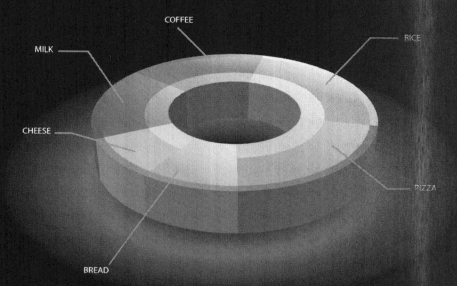

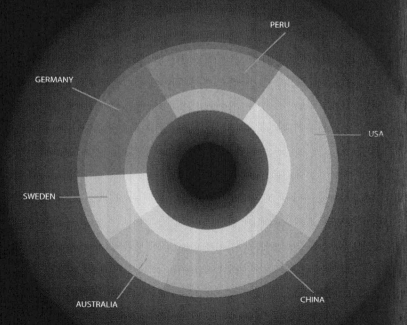

pie chart

WHAT IS IT?
A pie chart is a circle divided into sectors, illustrating proportion.

WHO INVENTED IT?
The earliest known pie chart is believed to be William Playfair's Statistical Breviary of 1801

WHY USE THIS METHOD?
1. The pie chart may be the most widely used statistical chart in business.

CHALLENGES
1. It is difficult to compare data between on or more pie charts.

RESOURCES
1. Pen
2. Paper
3. Compass
4. Protractor
5. Computer
6. Graphics software

WHEN TO USE THIS METHOD
1. Know Context
2. Know User
3. Frame insights

HOW TO USE THIS METHOD
1. Collect data from sources
2. Add the total
3. Calculate the percentage of the total each item.
4. Draw a circle
5. Draw a radius
6. Convert the percentages into angles
7. Each item will equal a percentage of the total and the same percentage of 360 degrees in a circle.
8. Each section is usually colored a different color
9. Label the sections of the pie chart.

REFERENCES
1. Cleveland, William S. (1985). The Elements of Graphing Data. Pacific Grove, CA: Wadsworth & Advanced Book Program. ISBN 0-534-03730-5.
2. Harris, Robert L. (1999). Information Graphics: A comprehensive Illustrated Reference. Oxford University Press. ISBN 0-19-513532-6.

POLARITIES MATRIX

POLARITIES	++	+	0	–	– –
PRICE					
CUSTOMER SERVICE					
QUALITY					
DELIVERY					
DESIGN					
ENVIRONMENTAL SUSTAINABILITY					
SERVICE					
DISTRIBUTION					
OPTIONS					
RELIABILITY					
PERFORMANCE					
BRAND					
INVESTMENT					
VISIBILITY					
SIMPLICITY					

• • • • • • • • • • • • • OUR PRODUCT

────────── COMPETITOR'S PRODUCT

Source: Haberfelner

polarities matrix

WHAT IS IT?
The polarities tool is a method of graphically comparing a number of alternatives.

WHY USE THIS METHOD?
1. It is used when there are a number of sub criteria to compare for a small number of options.
2. This method is used to compare factors related to a number of competitors.

REFERENCES
1. Olivier L. de Weck, Ernst Fricke, Siegfried Vössner Reinhard Haberfellner Orell Fuessli Verlag Systems Engineering (January 1, 2013) ISBN-10: 328004068X ISBN-13: 978-3280040683

WHEN TO USE THIS METHOD
1. Know Context
2. Know User
3. Frame insights

HOW TO USE THIS METHOD
1. Collect the required data.
2. Define a scale
3. Evaluate each criteria
4. Add each item to your graph

RESOURCES
1. Pen
2. Paper
3. Data

POWERGRAM

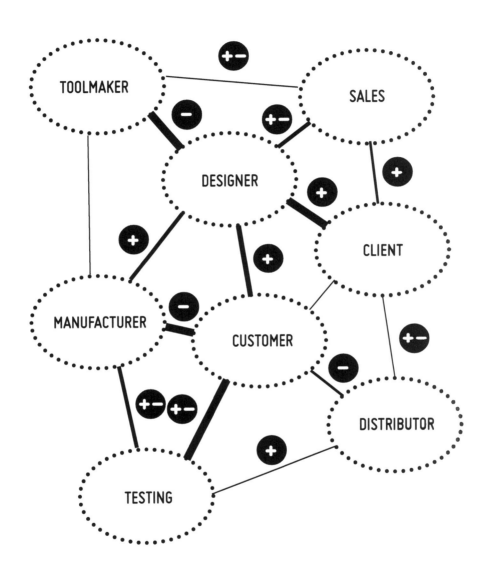

powergram

WHAT IS IT?

"A powergram is a graphical representation of the power dynamics, and power positions, within an account. It shows the true power structure, which is usually different than the account's organizational chart. It provides useful insights about an account's decision making process." *Source: Greg Alexander*

WHO INVENTED IT?

Greg Alexander

WHY USE THIS METHOD?

1. A more descriptive method than an organizational chart.
2. Can illustrate unofficial power structures.
3. Can be used to generate debate and discussion on roles and responsibilities.

CHALLENGES

1. Can be subjective.
2. Rank does not equal power.

WHEN TO USE THIS METHOD

1. Define intent
2. Know Context

HOW TO USE THIS METHOD

1. "Identify the formal lines of reporting and authority.
2. A circle represents a person
3. Identify the stakeholders you like to include
4. The larger the circle, the more power '
5. A line denotes a relationship
6. The heavier the line, the stronger the relationship
7. A strike through a line means a negative relationship
8. A shorter line represents a closer relationship,or frequent contact
9. A longer line represents a more distant the relationship"

Source: Greg Alexander

RESOURCES

1. Pen
2. Paper
3. Post-it-notes
4. White board
5. Dry erase pens

REFERENCES

1. Brill, Peter L. and Richard Worth. The four levers of corporate change. New York : AMACOM, 1997.

PROBLEM TREE

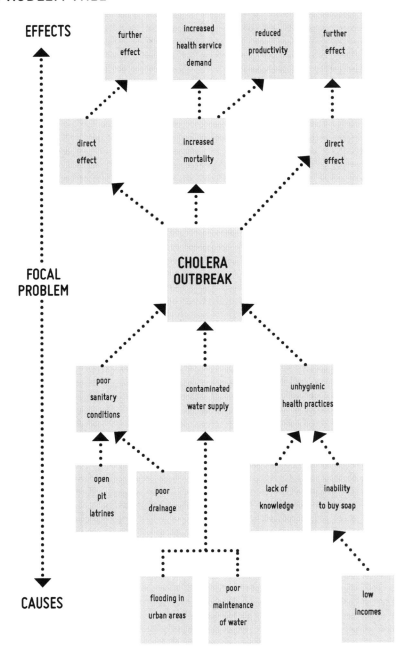

EFFECTS

further effect

increased health service demand

reduced productivity

further effect

direct effect

increased mortality

direct effect

FOCAL PROBLEM

CHOLERA OUTBREAK

poor sanitary conditions

contaminated water supply

unhygienic health practices

open pit latrines

poor drainage

lack of knowledge

inability to buy soap

CAUSES

flooding in urban areas

poor maintenance of water

low incomes

Source: Adapted from Water Supply and Sanitation Collaborative Council

problem tree

WHAT IS IT?

A problem tree is a tool for clarifying the problems being addressed by a design project. The problem tree shows a structured hierarchy of problems being addressed with higher level problems branching into related groups of sub-problems.

WHY USE THIS METHOD?

1. A problem tree is a visual way of mapping your design problems so that you can discuss and refine them.
2. It is useful for identify a core problem and it's and root causes
3. It is a way to refine vague problems into more concrete and solvable goals.
4. The problem tree often helps build a shared sense of understanding, purpose and action.

CHALLENGES

1. Consider the likely stakeholders and constraints.
2. It may be difficult to understand all effects and causes of a problem early in a project.

WHEN TO USE THIS METHOD

1. Define intent

HOW TO USE THIS METHOD

1. Imagine a large tree with its trunk, branches, leaves, primary and secondary roots.
2. Write the main problem/concern in the center of a large flip chart (trunk).
3. Add the causes of the main problem onto the chart below the main problem, with arrows leading to the problem (primary roots).
4. For each of the causes, write the factors that lead to them, again using arrows to show how each one contributes (secondary roots).
5. Draw arrows leading upwards from the main problem to the various effects/consequences of that problem (branches).
6. For each of these effects, add any further effects/consequences (leaves).

Source: Adapted from Water Supply and Sanitation Collaborative Council

RESOURCES

1. Pen
2. Paper
3. White board

REFERENCES

1. ODI (2009): Problem Tree Analysis. Successful Communication: Planning Tools. London: ODI
2. Campbell, K.l.i.; Garforth, C.; Heffernan, C.; Morton, J.; Paterson, R.; Rymer, C. ; Upton, M. (2006): The Problem Tree. Analysis of the causes and effects of problems. The Problem Tree. Analysis of the causes and effects of problems.

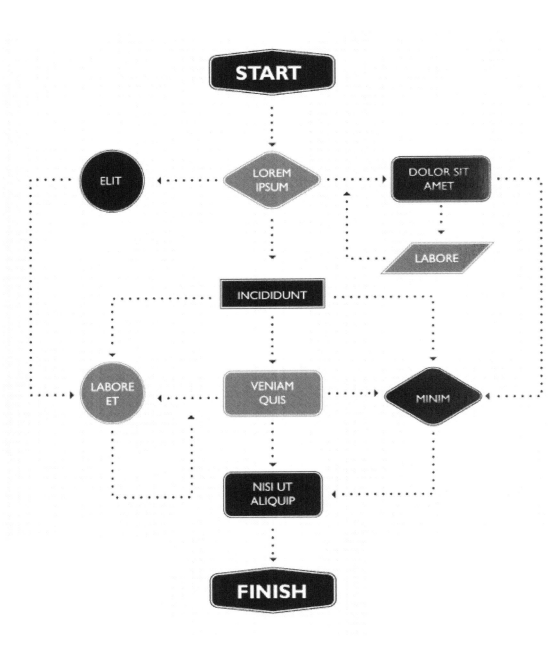

process flow diagram

WHAT IS IT?
A process flowchart is a type of diagram that represents a process, showing the steps as boxes

WHO INVENTED IT?
Frank Gilbreth, American Society of Mechanical Engineers,1921

WHY USE THIS METHOD?
1. To represent a flow of process or decisions or both.

CHALLENGES
1. Use standard symbols.
2. Arrows should show the direction of flow.
3. A junction is indicated by two incoming and one outgoing line.
4. The two most common types of boxes are for a process step and for a decisions.

RESOURCES
1. Pen
2. Paper
3. White board
4. Dry erase markers.

WHEN TO USE THIS METHOD
1. Know Context
2. Frame insights

HOW TO USE THIS METHOD
1. Define the process boundaries
2. Complete the big picture first.
3. Draw a start box.
4. Draw the first box below the start box. Ask, 'What happens first?'.
5. Add further boxes below the previous box, Ask 'What happens next?'.
6. Connect the boxes with arrows
7. Describe the process to be charted
8. Review.

REFERENCES
1. Frank Bunker Gilbreth, Lillian Moller Gilbreth (1921) Process Charts. American Society of Mechanical Engineers.
2. Bohl, Rynn: "Tools for Structured and Object-Oriented Design", Prentice Hall, 2007.

PRODUCT LIFECYCLE MAP

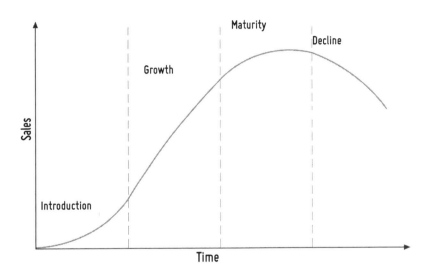

product life cycle map

WHAT IS IT?
A product lifecycle map shows the sales of a product over time. there are four stages in the life of a product, the introduction stage, the growth stage, the maturity stage and the decline stage.

WHO INVENTED IT?
Geoffrey Moore 1991

WHY USE THIS METHOD?
1. For strategic planning

CHALLENGES
1. The performance of each product will not be the same so review the performance of a product category.

WHEN TO USE THIS METHOD
1. Define intent
2. Frame insights

HOW TO USE THIS METHOD
1. Collect data
2. Map data
3. Project data

RESOURCES
1. Pen
2. Paper
3. White board
4. Dry erase markers.

REFERENCES
1. Karnie, Arie; Reich, Yoram (2011). Managing the Dynamic of New Product Development Processes. A new Product Lifecycle Management Paradigm. Springer. p. 13. ISBN 978-0-85729-569-9.
2. Saaksvuori, Antti (2008). Product Lifecycle Management. Springer. ISBN 978-3-540-78173-8.
3. Stark, John (2006). Global Product: Strategy, Product Lifecycle Management and the Billion Customer Question. Springer. ISBN 978-1-84628-915-6.

CRITERIA	CONCEPT 1	CONCEPT 2	CONCEPT 3	CONCEPT 4
Functionality	S	-	-	+
Cost	+	+	+	+
Aesthetics	-	S	-	+
Manufacturability	-	+	+	-
Usability	+	+	-	S
Safety	-	-	-	-
Reliability	-	S	-	-
Maintenance	+	-	-	S
Efficiency	+	+	S	+
Environmental Impact	-	+	-	-
Speed to market	S	-	+	-
Fit with Brand	+	+	-	-
TOTAL	0	2	-3	-2

97

pugh's matrix

WHAT IS IT?
Pugh's Method is a design evaluation method that uses criteria in an evaluation matrix to compare alternative design directions.

WHO INVENTED IT?
Stuart Pugh 1977

WHY USE THIS METHOD?
1. Overcome shortcomings of design
2. Find different ideas to satisfy criteria
3. Explore alternatives
4. This method can make subjective observations more objective.

CHALLENGES
1. Groupthink
2. Not enough good ideas
3. Taking turns
4. Freeloading
5. Inhibition
6. Lack of critical thinking
7. A group that is too large competes for attention.

WHEN TO USE THIS METHOD
1. Know Context
2. Know User
3. Frame insights
4. Explore Concepts
5. Make Plans

HOW TO USE THIS METHOD
1. Develop the evaluation criteria
2. Identify design criteria to be compared.
3. Design concepts: original design
4. Concepts brainstormed
5. Evaluation matrix: each design evaluated against a best design datum
6. Generate Scores.
7. Calculate the total score
8. Iterate, refine, optimize design
9. Document results

EVALUATION SCALE
+ means substantially better
– means clearly worse
S means more or less the same

RESOURCES
1. White board
2. Dry-erase markers
3. Pens
4. Paper
5. Design Team, 4 to 12 cross disciplinary members
6. Room with privacy

REFERENCES
1. Stuart Pugh, Don Clausing, Ron Andrade, (April 24, 1996). Creating Innovative Products Using Total Design. Addison Wesley Longman. ISBN 0-201-63485-6
2. S. Pugh (1981) Concept selection: a method that works. In: Hubka, V. (ed.), Review of design methodology. Proceedings interna¬tional conference on engineering design, March 1981, Rome. Zürich: Heurista, 1981, blz. 497 — 506.

RADAR CHART

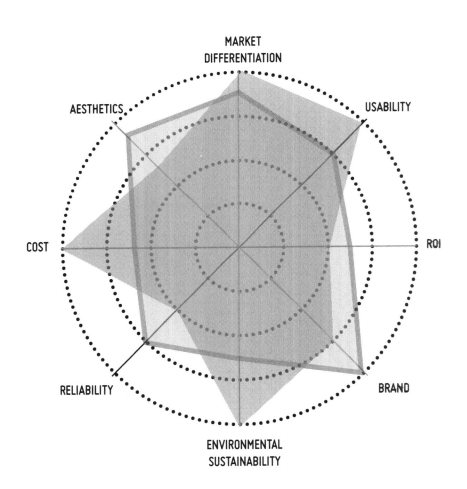

radar chart

WHAT IS IT?

The radar chart is a star shape chart that allows information to be logged radially for a number of variables. The radar chart is also known as a web chart, spider chart, star chart, star plot, cobweb chart, irregular polygon, polar chart, or kiviat diagram.

WHO INVENTED IT?

Georg von Mayr 1877

CHALLENGES

1.   Radar charts may not provide information for trade off decisions.

WHY USE THIS METHOD?

1.   A spider diagram is a way of displaying a great deal of information in a condensed form,

WHEN TO USE THIS METHOD

1.   Know Context
2.   Know User
3.   Frame insights

HOW TO USE THIS METHOD

1.   Draw a circle on a flipchart paper
2.   For each item to evaluate draw a line from the center to the circle.
3.   Write the item on the intersection between the line and the circle.
4.   Draw spider lines from the inside to the outside of the circle (see photo).
5.   Gather the participants around the flipchart.
6.   Ask them to put one dot for each item: If highly ranked the dot should be close top the center; if poorly ranked the dot should be close to the circle.
7.   Present and discuss the result with the group.

RESOURCES

1.   Paper
2.   Pens
3.   Computer
4.   Graphic software

REFERENCES

1.   Chambers, John, William Cleveland, Beat Kleiner, and Paul Tukey, (1983). Graphical Methods for Data Analysis. Wadsworth. pp. 158-162

REFRAMING MATRIX

PRODUCT PERSPECTIVE

1. Is there something wrong with the product or service?
2. Is it priced correctly?
3. How well does it serve the market?
4. Is it reliable?

PLANNING PERSPECTIVE

1. Are our business plans, marketing plans, or strategy at fault?
2. Could we improve these?

POTENTIAL PERSPECTIVE

1. How would we increase sales?
2. If we were to seriously increase our targets or our production volumes, what would happen with this problem?

PEOPLE PERSPECTIVE

1. What are the people impacts and people implications of the problem?
2. What do people involved with the problem think?
3. Why are customers not using or buying the product?

DESIGN PROBLEM ···

···

reframing matrix

WHAT IS IT?

The reframing matrix is a method of approaching a problem by imagining the perspectives of a number of different people and exploring the possible solutions that they might suggest.

WHO INVENTED IT?

Michael Morgan 1993

WHY USE THIS METHOD?

1. This is a method for assisting in empathy which is an important factor in gaining acceptance and creating successful design.

CHALLENGES

1. The reframing is not done with stakeholders present or in context so may be subjective

RESOURCES

1. Pens
2. Paper
3. Post it notes
4. White board
5. Dry erase markers

WHEN TO USE THIS METHOD

1. Define intent

HOW TO USE THIS METHOD

1. Define a problem.
2. On a white board or paper draw a large square and divide it into four quadrants.
3. Select 4 different perspectives to approach the problem. They could be four professions or four people or four other perspectives that are important for your problem.
4. With your team brainstorm a number of questions that you believe are important from the perspectives that you have selected.
5. The moderator writes the questions in the relevant quadrants of the matrix.
6. The group discusses each of these questions.
7. The answers are recorded and the perspectives are incorporated into the considerations for design solutions.

REFERENCES

1. Morgan, M. Creating Workforce Innovation: Turning Individual Creativity into Organizational Innovation. Publisher: Business & Professional Pub (October 1993) ISBN-10: 1875680020 ISBN-13: 978-1875680023

RISK MAP

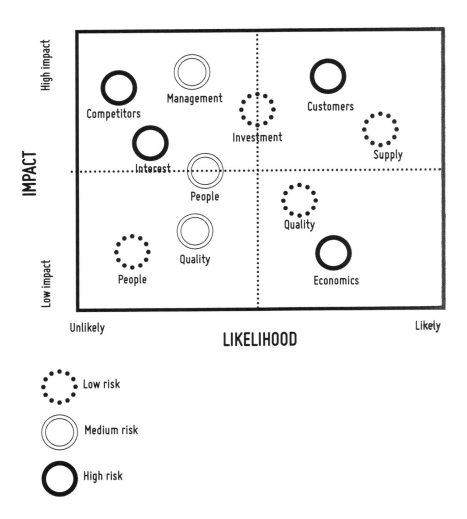

risk map

WHAT IS IT?

A risk map is a method of analyzing risk in order to understand which risks may require action or strategy to control.

WHY USE THIS METHOD?

1. To identify risks
2. To exploit opportunities
3. To control the impact of risks.

RESOURCES

1. Pen
2. Paper
3. White board
4. Dry erase markers
5. Post-it notes

REFERENCES

1. Crockford, Neil (1986). An Introduction to Risk Management (2 ed.). Cambridge, UK: Woodhead-Faulkner. p. 18. ISBN 0-85941-332-2.
2. Flyvbjerg, B., 2006, ""From Nobel Prize to Project Management: Getting Risks Right." Project Management Journal, vol. 37, no. 3, August 2006, pp. 5-15.

WHEN TO USE THIS METHOD

1. Define intent
2. Frame insights
3. Explore Concepts

HOW TO USE THIS METHOD

1. Collect primary research through qualitative and quantitative methods such as focus groups or questionnaires.
2. Collect secondary research data.
3. Analyze data.
4. Create a list of risk issues using the headings: process, people, requirements, schedule, cost, environment, and others.
5. Draw a risk map graphing each by the perception of whether it is controllable or not controllable and observable or not observable.
6. Crete a second map and plot each risk by the likely impact and how likely the risk event is to occur.
7. Identify ways to reduce risks
8. Prioritize risk reduction strategies.
9. Be transparent and inclusive
10. Continually re-assess risk

RISK REWARD ANALYSIS

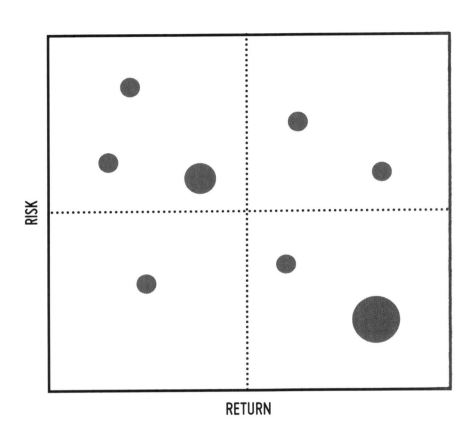

risk reward analysis

WHAT IS IT?
A risk-reward analysis is a method to assess the risk and reward of a number of different ideas.

WHY USE THIS METHOD?
1. For comparing different strategic directions for the company.
2. For deciding which projects to keep within the program and which to discard.
3. Use by an individual team member deciding how best to spend their day.

WHEN TO USE THIS METHOD
1. Define intent
2. Frame insights
3. Explore Concepts
4. Make Plans

HOW TO USE THIS METHOD
1. Create a list of all the different options and their possible rewards.
2. Plot the alternatives on the risk-reward chart.
3. The bigger the bubble the more resources are required to execute that option.
4. Analyze the chart to determine where the best balance of risk and reward is to be found.

RESOURCES
1. Pen
2. Paper
3. White board
4. Dry erase markers
5. Post-it notes

smart goals

WHAT IS IT?
SMART is a method of setting objectives.

WHY USE THIS METHOD?
1. SMART is a thorough and effective way of setting goals for a project.

WHO INVENTED IT?
George T. Doran 1981

WHEN TO USE THIS METHOD
1. Define intent

RESOURCES
1. White board
2. Dry-erase markers.
3. Paper
4. Pens

REFERENCES
1. Doran, G. T. (1981). There's a S.M.A.R.T. way to write management's goals and objectives. Management Review, Volume 70, Issue 11(AMA FORUM), pp. 35-36.

HOW TO USE THIS METHOD
1. Brainstorm with your team the goals of the project using the SMART mnemonic.
2. A moderator can list the headings on a white board and team members can contribute individual goals using post-it-notes.
3. A specific goal will usually answer the five "W" questions: what,why, where, when, which.
4. Letter: S. Major term Specific. Minor terms Significant, Stretching, Simple
5. Letter M Major term Measurable Minor term Meaningful, Motivational, Manageable
6. Letter: A. Major term Attainable. Minor terms: Appropriate, Achievable, Agreed, Assignable, Actionable, Adjustable, Ambitious, Aligned, Aspirational, Acceptable, Action-focused
7. Letter: R. Major term Relevant. Minor terms Result-Based, Results-oriented, Resourced, Resonant, Realistic
8. Letter: T. Major term Timely. Minor terms Time-oriented, Time framed, Timed, Time-based, Timeboxed, Time-bound, Time-Specific, Timetabled, Time limited, Trackable, Tangible

SOCIOGRAM

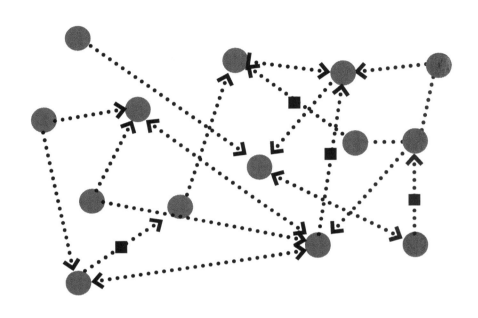

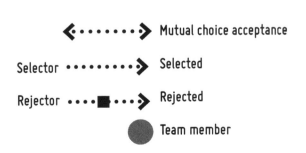

Mutual choice acceptance

Selector ··········> Selected

Rejector ····■····> Rejected

Team member

sociogram

WHAT IS IT?
A sociogram is a map of team interactions and structure. It is used to foster partnerships, team cohesiveness and participation.

WHO INVENTED IT?
J. L. Moreno 1934

WHY USE THIS METHOD?
1. A sociogram identifies alliances within the group.

REFERENCES
1. "An Experiential Approach to Organization Development 7th ed."Brown, Donald R.and Harvey, Don. Page 134

WHEN TO USE THIS METHOD
1. Define intent
2. Frame insights
3. Deliver Offering

HOW TO USE THIS METHOD
1. The moderator performs ongoing team observations.
2. Notes are recorded on team observations
3. A sociogram is drawn and shared with the team.
4. An open discussion follows on ways to improve the team's interactions and performance.
5. The team and moderator develop a strategy for improving team performance and interactions.

RESOURCES
1. Paper
2. Pens
3. White board
4. Dry erase markers

STAKEHOLDER MAP

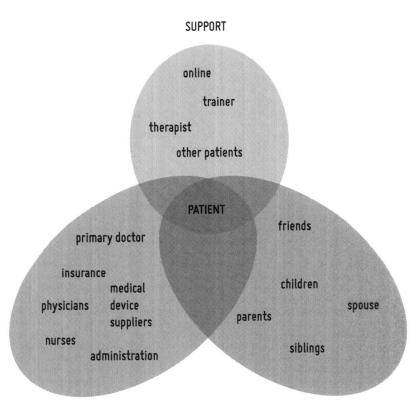

SUPPORT

online

trainer

therapist

other patients

PATIENT

primary doctor

friends

insurance

children

medical
physicians   device   spouse
suppliers
parents

nurses

administration

siblings

HEALTH CARE

FAMILY & FRIENDS

stakeholder map

WHAT IS IT?
Stakeholders maps are used to document the key stake holders and their relationship. They can include end users, those who will benefit, those who may be adversely affected, those who hold power and those who may sabotage design outcomes. At the beginning of a design project it is important to identify the key stake holders and their relationships. The map serves as a reference for the design team.

WHO INVENTED IT?
Mitchell 1997

WHY USE THIS METHOD?
1. Stakeholder mapping helps discover ways to influence other stakeholders.
2. Stakeholder mapping helps discover risks.
3. Stakeholder mapping helps discover positive stakeholders to involve in the design process.

CHALLENGES?
1. Stakeholder mapping helps discover negative stakeholders and their associated risks.

RESOURCES
1. White board
2. Post-it-notes
3. Pens
4. Dry-erase markers
5. Interview data

WHEN TO USE THIS METHOD
1. Define intent
2. Know Context
3. Know User
4. Frame insights

HOW TO USE THIS METHOD
1. Develop a categorized list of the members of the stakeholder community.
2. Assign priorities
3. Map the 'highest priority' stakeholders.
4. Can initially be documented on a white board, cards, post-it-notes and consolidated as a diagram through several iterations showing hierarchy and relationships.

Some of the commonly used 'dimensions' include:
1. Power (three levels)
2. Support (three levels)
3. Influence (three levels)
4. Need (three levels)

REFERENCES
1. Mitchell, R. K., B. R. Agle, and D.J. Wood. (1997). "Toward a Theory of Stakeholder Identification and Salience: Defining the Principle of Who and What really Counts." in: Academy of Management Review 22(4): 853 - 888
2. Savage, G. T., T. W. Nix, Whitehead and Blair. (1991). "Strategies for assessing and managing organizational stakeholders." In: Academy of Management Executive 5(2): 61 — 75.

INTERNAL STAKEHOLDERS

FUNCTION	NAME 1	NAME 2	NAME 3	NAME 4
MARKETING				
SALES				
CUST. SERVICE				
HR				
IT				
ENGINEERING				
DESIGN				
MANAGEMENT				
FINANCE				
EMPLOYEES				
REPS				

Out of scope ☐   In scope ▒   Highest priority ▓

EXTERNAL STAKEHOLDERS

FUNCTION	NAME 1	NAME 2	NAME 3	NAME 4
COMPETITORS				
GOVERNMENT				
CUSTOMERS				
SUPPLIERS				
MEDIA				
CLIENTS				

stakeholder scope map

WHAT IS IT?
A stakeholder scope map is a map that indicates the priority and scope of stakeholders in a project

WHO INVENTED IT?
Mel Silberman 2000

WHY USE THIS METHOD?
1. The map assists in identifying which stakeholders should be given priority during a project.

CHALLENGES
1. Should not be too detailed

REFERENCES
1. The Consultant's Toolkit: High-Impact Questionnaires, Activities and How-to. Guides for Diagnosing and Solving Client Problems, Mel Silberman (2000)

WHEN TO USE THIS METHOD
1. Define intent

HOW TO USE THIS METHOD
1. Brainstorm with your design team a list of internal stakeholders and a list of external stakeholders.
2. Determine which stakeholders are highest priority and which stakeholders are inside and outside the scope of the project management process.
3. Identify conflicts of interest.

RESOURCES
1. Pens
2. Paper
3. White board
4. Dry erase markers
5. Post-it-notes

SUSTAINABILITY MAP

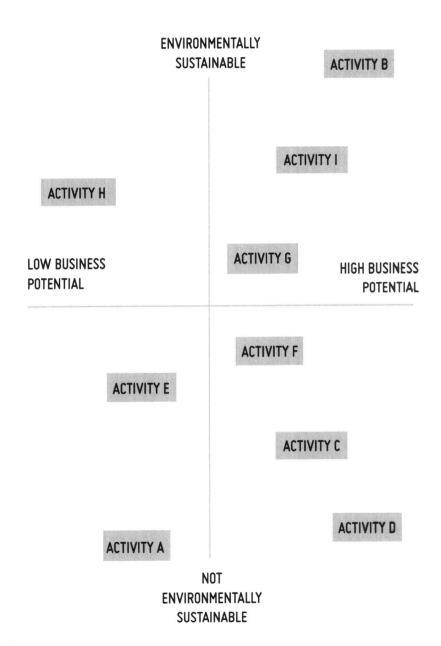

sustainability map

WHAT IS IT?

This method allows the team to assess the relative business potential and environmental impact of products and services.

WHY USE THIS METHOD?

1. Aids communication and discussion within the organization.
2. To gain competitive advantage with environmental sustainability,
3. Helps build competitive strategy
4. Helps build team alignment

CHALLENGES

1. Can be subjective

WHEN TO USE THIS METHOD

1. Know Context
2. Know User
3. Frame insights
4. Explore Concepts

HOW TO USE THIS METHOD

1. Moderator draws grid on whiteboard or flip chart.
2. Team brainstorms
3. Interpret the map.
4. Create strategy.
5. Products and services which have both high environmental sustainability and good business proposition are given priority.

RESOURCES

1. Pen
2. Paper
3. White board
4. Dry erase markers

SWIMLANES

ACTIVITY PHASE	CUSTOMER ACTIONS	TOUCHPOINTS	LINE OF INTERACTION	DIRECT CONTACT	LINE OF VISIBILITY	BACK OFFICE	EMOTIONAL EXPERIENCE
							+
							−

swimlanes

WHAT IS IT?

Diagram that shows parallel streams for user, business, and technical process flows. You can include a storyboard lane. Create a blueprint for each persona, interaction or scenario. Provides a focus for discussion and refinement of services or experiences. They may document activities over time such as:

1. Customer Actions
2. Touch points
3. Direct Contact visible to customers
4. Invisible back office actions
5. Support Processes
6. Physical Evidence
7. Emotional Experience for customer.

WHO INVENTED IT?

Lynn Shostack 1983

WHY USE THIS METHOD?

1. Can be used for design or improvement of existing services or experiences.
2. Is more tangible than intuition.
3. Makes the process of service development more efficient.
4. A common point of reference for stakeholders for planning and discussion.
5. Tool to assess the impact of change.

WHEN TO USE THIS METHOD

1. Know Context
2. Know User
3. Frame insights

HOW TO USE THIS METHOD

1. Define the service or experience to focus on.
2. A blueprint can be created in a brainstorming session with stakeholders.
3. Define the customer demographic.
4. See though the customer's eyes.
5. Define the activities and phases of activity under each heading.
6. Link the contact or customer touchpoints to the needed support functions
7. Use post-it-notes on a white board for initial descriptions and rearrange as necessary drawing lines to show the links.
8. Create the blueprint then refine iteratively.

RESOURCES

1. Paper
2. Pens
3. White board
4. Dry-erase markers
5. Camera
6. Blueprint templates
7. Post-it-notes

REFERENCES

1. (1991) G. Hollins, W. Hollins, Total Design: Managing the design process in the service sector, Trans Atlantic Publications
2. (2004) R. Kalakota, M.Robinson, Services Blueprint: Roadmap for Execution, Addison-Wesley, Boston.

VENN DIAGRAM

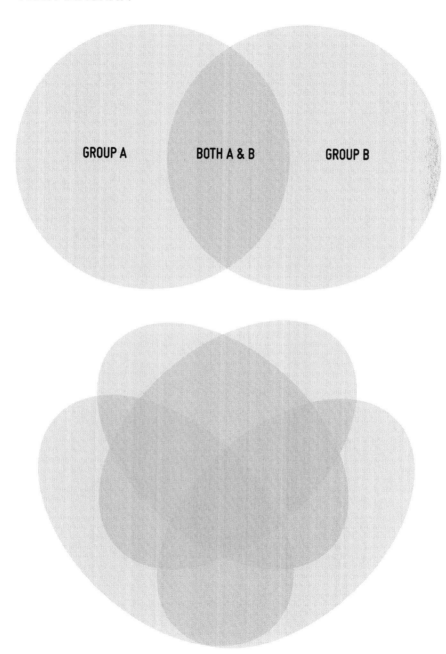

GROUP A   BOTH A & B   GROUP B

Venn's four-set diagram using ellipses

venn diagram

WHAT IS IT?
Venn diagrams normally are constructed from overlapping circles. The interior of the circle and the areas of overlap symbolically represents the elements of discreet sets.

WHO INVENTED IT?
John Venn 1880

WHY USE THIS METHOD?
1. A useful tool for simplifying and communicating data related to user populations and design features

WHEN TO USE THIS METHOD
1. Know Context
2. Know User
3. Frame insights

RESOURCES
1. Paper
2. Pens
3. Software

REFERENCES
1. Grimaldi, Ralph P. (2004). Discrete and combinatorial mathematics. Boston: Addison-Wesley. p. 143. ISBN 0-201-72634-3.
2. Edwards, A.W.F. (2004). Cogwheels of the mind: the story of Venn diagrams. JHU Press. ISBN 978-0-8018-7434-5.

WORD DIAMOND

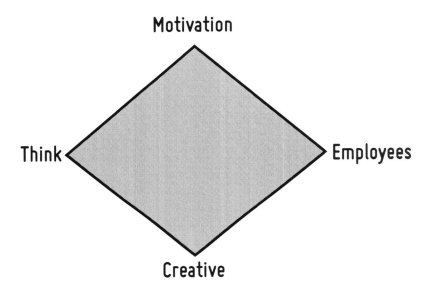

Source: Elspeth McFadzean

word diamond

WHAT IS IT?

Word Diamond is a technique developed in order to generate ideas from the problem statement.

WHO INVENTED IT?

VanGundy 1992

WHY USE THIS METHOD?

1. This exercise can be performed by anyone.
2. Does not require an experienced group or moderator.

RESOURCES

1. Paper
2. Pens
3. White board
4. Dry erase markers
5. Post-it-notes

REFERENCES

1. Encouraging Creative Thinking Author: Elspeth McFadzean, Henley Management College, Henley-on-Thames, UK First published: 2000

WHEN TO USE THIS METHOD

1. Define intent
2. Frame insights
3. Explore Concepts

HOW TO USE THIS METHOD

1. "The group participants choose four words or phrases from the problem statement.
2. These words can then be placed in a diamond shape so that each word or phrase lies at one of the points.
3. The group participants are asked to combine the words or phrases together and to tell the facilitator the ideas that have occurred due to the combination. The facilitator writes the ideas down on a flip chart.
4. Next, the two words, which were initially selected, are combined with a third word to develop more ideas.
5. Steps 3 and 4 are repeated until all possible combinations are examined and all the ideas have been recorded.
6. The group continues to combine words and record ideas until they have exhausted all possibilities. These ideas can then be analyzed and developed into workable solutions"

Source: VanGundy 1992

index

E

F

G

H

I

J

K

L

index

Other titles from this author

Design Methods 1
200 ways to apply design thinking
Author: Curedale, Robert A
Publisher: Design Community College, Inc.
Edition 1 November 2013
ISBN-10:0988236206
ISBN-13:978-0-9882362-0-2

Design Methods 2
200 more ways to apply design thinking
Author: Curedale, Robert A
Publisher: Design Community College, Inc.
Edition 1 January 2013
ISBN-13: 978-0988236240
ISBN-10: 0988236249

Design Research Methods
150 ways to inform design
Author: Curedale, Robert A
Publisher: Design Community College, Inc.
Edition 1 January 2013
ISBN-10: 0988236257
ISBN-13: 978-0-988-2362-5-7

50 Brainstorming Methods
Author: Curedale, Robert A
Publisher: Design Community College, Inc.
Edition 1 January 2013
ISBN-10: 0988236230
ISBN-13: 978-0-9882362-3-3

50 Selected Design Methods
to inform your design
Author: Curedale, Robert A
Publisher: Design Community College, Inc.
Edition 1 January 2013
ISBN-10:0988236265
ISBN-13:978-0-9882362-6-4

Design Thinking
Process and Methods Manual
Author: Curedale, Robert A
Publisher: Design Community College, Inc.
Edition 1 April 2013
ISBN-10:0988236249
ISBN-13: 978-0-9882362-4-0

about the author

Rob Curedale was born in Australia and worked as a designer, director and educator in leading design offices in London, Sydney, Switzerland, Portugal, Los Angeles, Silicon Valley, Detroit, and China. He designed and managed over 1,000 products and experiences as a consultant and in-house design leader for the world's most respected brands. Rob has three decades experience in every aspect of product development, leading design teams to achieve transformational improvements in operating and financial results. He has extensive experience in forging strategic growth, competitive advantage, and a background in expanding business into emerging markets through user advocacy and extensive cross cultural expertise. Rob's designs can be found in millions of homes and workplaces around the world.

Rob works currently as a Adjunct Professor at Art Center College of Design in Pasadena and consults to organizations in the United States and internationally and presents workshops related to design. He has taught as a member of staff and presented lectures and workshops at many respected design schools and universities throughout the world including Yale, Pepperdine University, Art Center Pasadena, Loyola University, Cranbrook, Pratt, Art Center Europe; a faculty member at SCA and UTS Sydney; as Chair of Product Design and Furniture Design at the College for Creative Studies in Detroit, then the largest product design school in North America, Art Institute Hollywood, Cal State San Jose, Escola De Artes e Design in Oporto Portugal, Instituto De Artes Visuals, Design e Marketing, Lisbon, Southern Yangtze University, Jiao Tong University in Shanghai and Nanjing Arts Institute in China.

Rob's design practice experience includes projects for HP, Philips, GEC, Nokia, Sun, Apple, Canon, Motorola, Nissan, Audi VW, Disney, RTKL, Governments of the UAE,UK, Australia, Steelcase, Hon, Castelli, Hamilton Medical, Zyliss, Belkin, Gensler, Haworth, Honeywell, NEC, Hoover, Packard Bell, Dell, Black & Decker, Coleman and Harmon Kardon. Categories including furniture, healthcare, consumer electronics, sporting, homewares, military, exhibits, packaging. His products and experiences can be found in millions of homes and businesses throughout the world.

Rob established and manages the largest network of designers and architects in the world with more than 300,000 professional members working in every field of design.